# The Soledad Children

## The Fight to End Discriminatory IQ Tests

Marty Glick + Maurice Jourdane

ARTE
PÚBLICO
PRESS

*Recovering the past, creating the future*

Arte Público Press
University of Houston
4902 Gulf Fwy, Bldg 19, Rm 100
Houston, Texas 77204-2004

Cover design by Mora Des!gn

Names: Glick, Marty, author. | Jourdane, Maurice, author.
Title: The Soledad children : the fight to end discriminatory IQ tests / by Marty Glick and Maurice Jourdane.
Description: Houston, Texas : Arte Publico Press, 2019. | Summary: "Ten-year-old Arturo Velazquez was born and raised on a farm labor camp in Soledad, California. He was bright and gregarious, but he didn't speak English when he started first grade. When he entered third grade in 1968, the psychologist at Soledad Elementary School gave him an English-language IQ test. Based on the results, he was placed in a class for the "Educable Mentally Retarded (EMR)." Arturo wasn't the only Spanish-speaking child in the room; all but one were from farmworker families. All were devastated by the stigma and lack of opportunity to learn. In 1969, attorneys at California Rural Legal Assistance (CRLA) discovered California public schools were misusing English-language, culturally biased IQ tests, by asking questions like "Who wrote Romeo and Juliet?" to place Spanish-speaking students into EMR classes. Additionally, Mexican-American children were not the only minorities impacted. While African-American and Mexican-American students made up 21.5% of the state population, they were 48% of special education programs! Written by two of the attorneys who led the charge against the unjust denial of an education to Mexican-American youth, The Soledad Children: The Fight to End Discriminatory IQ Tests recounts the history of both the CRLA and the class-action suit filed in 1970, Diana v. the State Board of Education, on behalf of 13,000 Hispanic kids already placed in EMR classes and another 100,000 at risk of being relegated to a virtual purgatory. From securing removal from EMR classes for the misplaced to ensuring revised, appropriate testing for students throughout the state, this engrossing book recounts the historic struggle-by lawyers, parents, psychologists and legislators-to guarantee all affected young people in California received equitable access to education"—Provided by publisher.
Identifiers: LCCN 2019028871 (print) | LCCN 2019028872 (ebook) | ISBN 9781558858886 (paperback) | ISBN 9781518505874 (epub) | ISBN 9781518505881 (kindle edition) | ISBN 9781518505898 (adobe pdf)
Subjects: LCSH: California. State Board of Education,—Trials, litigation, etc. | Special education—Law and legislation—California—Soledad—History—20th century—Cases. | Intelligence tests—Law and legislation—California—Soledad—History—20th century—Cases. | Educational tests and measurements—Law and legislation—California—Soledad—History—20th century | Discrimination in education—Law and legislation—California—Soledad—History—20th century—Cases. | Mexican American children—Legal status, laws, etc.—California—Soledad—History—20th century—Cases. | California Rural Legal Assistance Foundation.
Classification: LCC KF228.D498 G55 2019 (print) | LCC KF228.D498 (ebook) | DDC 344.73/0798—dc23
LC record available at https://lccn.loc.gov/2019028871
LC ebook record available at https://lccn.loc.gov/2019028872

19  20  21  22          5  4  3  2  1

*To the determined and fearless parents of Arturo, Diana, Manuel Jr., María, Ramón, Margarita, Armando, Rachel and Ernesto—The Soledad Children.*

# TABLE OF CONTENTS

# ACKNOWLEDGEMENTS

We wish to acknowledge California Rural Legal Assistance and their legal services program attorneys, community workers and staff who for over fifty years have devoted their time and energy, often for below market wages, to vital representation of low income individuals and persons of color who could not afford attorneys.

We especially thank Manny Dumalag and Terry Metasavage for their invaluable assistance in helping to process, edit, format and assemble the manuscript and Nicolas Kanellos at Arte Público Press who provided invaluable guidance and tough but critical editing. The Arte Público staff, Gabriela Baeza Ventura and Marina Tristán, patiently worked with us to make our book better and guide it to publication and promotion and we thank them. Kudos to our publicist—Marissa DeCuir, Angelle Barbazon and the staff of JKS Communications for their hard work in spreading the word about *The Soledad Children*. Bev Glick provided her keen eye in the editing process as did Joanie Chevalier. The kind words, encouragement and input from Luis Valdez, Judge Thelton Henderson and Maria Louisa Alaniz are most appreciated.

Many individuals gave of their time be interviewed so we want to acknowledge their important input and help. They include Uvaldo Palomares, Manual Reyes, Ramon Racio, Hector de la Rosa, Armando Menocal, Carlos Bowker, Jose Padilla, Bob Gnaizda, Gene Livingston, and Alejandro Matuk. Standing very tall in our memory are Federal Judge Robert F Peckham and former state senator and Congressman Clair Burgener of San Diego. We also are appreciative of the vintage photos provided by Bill Daniels.

Finally, we wish to thank and acknowledge our wives, Bev Glick and Olivia Jourdane and our own children, Alex G, Jonathan J, Jackie J and Jonathan G, for their support, patience and encouragement to tell the story, an endeavor that began in 2005 and continued in earnest from 2015-19.

# AUTHOR'S NOTE

We commenced writing and documenting the events por-
trayed and discussed in *The Soledad Children* in 2005 and it was,
on and off in the years that followed, a labor of both diligence and
love until we completed it in 2018. Fortunately, in retelling the
important events described in our book, we had access to the
entire court file for the *Diana and Larry P.* cases. We also had con-
temporaneous notes, summaries and files from the 1960s as well
as newspaper accounts from the time that we had saved. CRLA
back at the time published an in-house newsletter—*Noticiarios*—
four times a year, and those gave accounts of major cases. Of
course we have our own recollections, some vivid, and we were
fortunate to be able to interview several others who were involved
in the events at the time. The words used in conversations from
some five decades ago are as we recall them. While they may not
be precise, they reflect our recollections of the tenor and sub-
stance. The events presented all occurred and did so in the order
we present them. (Thanks also to search engines that are invaluable for establishing chronology and yielding such gems as old
newspaper accounts and dates of relevant history.) We, very occasionally and deliberately, changed a name or ascribed a comment
in a way to respect privacy. Otherwise, we diligently presented the
facts to be as accurate as possible to the best of our ability.

# PROLOGUE

Arturo Velázquez, born and raised in a farm labor camp in the small, wind-blown town of Soledad, California, turned ten in the Fall of 1968. The labor camp was bleak; its decaying small houses had served during World War II as a prison camp for captured German soldiers shipped to Soledad from the European theatre to provide convict labor for the growers. The chain link fence that had contained the German POWs still surrounded the camp, except where it had worn through or been cut to make a shortcut.

Arturo was bright, gregarious and energetic. He watched the San Francisco 49ers play on the family's second-hand, RCA Victor twelve-inch television and learned the players' names. He loved listening to his father talk with pride about *El Tri* (the three colors of the flag), the Mexican national soccer team that had bested both Columbia and Spain at the 1968 summer Olympics. Arturo practiced his kicks into a makeshift goal in the camp. He had never been further from home than Salinas, thirty miles away to the north. He was raised speaking only Spanish. School for Arturo was as suppressive as the woven wire fence around his labor camp home.

Arturo's parents, Francisco and Viviente, both born in Veracruz, Mexico, had labored since they were children as farmworkers in the United States. The Velázquez family had traveled from field to field in Texas, Arizona and California; like hundreds of thousands of other migrants they weeded, thinned, irrigated and harvested for low wages the fruits and vegetables that are the basis of California's $40 billion-a-year agricultural industry. It is an industry that produces, sells and ships two-thirds of the country's fruit and nuts and one-third of its vegetables.

In the early 1950s, Francisco and Viviente had applied for and obtained Green Cards and, in 1955, they settled in Soledad. Francisco could no longer handle the rigors of farm labor but had found a job as a tractor mechanic. Viviente and the five older children in the family still spent hot days weeding and thinning in the summer and picking and boxing green lettuce and broccoli in the fields during the fall harvest. The Velázquez family spoke Spanish at home, on the job and in their labor camp community. They taught their children the only language they spoke.

Arturo was actually looking forward to starting school. When he entered the first grade, he neither spoke nor understood any English. His teachers at the elementary school in East Soledad spoke only English in their classes. As far as Arturo could tell, none of his teachers or their occasional class assistants spoke or comprehended Spanish, except for a few common words. Thus, Arturo understood little of his first two years of instruction, but began to pick up English from some of his classmates and from his books. Over the summer, when not working at chores and helping out in the fields, Arturo worked to learn more English from television programs and from his second-hand reading book. Sometimes he practiced in front of a mirror. Arturo knew he would do better in his third year. It had been difficult, and he knew he was well behind the Anglo kids.

Arturo had never learned grammar or spelling, not even in Spanish. Arturo liked arithmetic but was shy. Like most migrant farmworker children, he was assigned a seat in the very back of the classroom. He never raised his hand nor spoke up, even when he thought he knew the answer to a question. His teachers simply ignored him, as well the other children of Mexican-American farmworkers.

When Arturo arrived at the Soledad Main Street Elementary School on an early September morning for the third grade, he joined the other children streaming past the solitary tree in the front yard into the white stucco, one-story elementary schoolhouse. At that time, the Main Street School housed students from kindergarten through eighth grade. Arturo and his friends exchanged *holas*, and he went down the long hallway to his classroom. When he got there, a teacher taking attendance stopped him.

"Hello, Arthur. Please head down the hall to Room 7. We need to give you a little test before you go to school today."

"A test? Now?" Arturo said. "But we have no classes yet."

"It is only to see what you have learned. Don't worry," the teacher said as she turned to check off the name of the next child.

Arturo found Room 7, a classroom with no other students. Sitting in front was an Anglo man with a white beard. The man was looking down at papers on his desk and had not yet noticed the small boy.

Arturo cleared his voice, "Hello, I am Arturo. They tell me to come here."

The school psychologist looked up and gestured at a seat in the second row. "Oh, yes. You must be Arthur Velázquez. I'll be with you in a minute. Sit here." The man continued making marks on some papers, ignoring Arturo for what seemed like a long time.

Arturo sat there, getting more nervous as time passed in silence.

Finally, the man came over and asked, "Arthur, you speak English?"

"My name is Arturo. I am learning English."

"Good to hear that, Arthur," said the man briskly. "We have a special test for you to take today. It will help you out. Do your best."

Then the stranger handed Arturo what turned out to be the Weschler IQ test, but did not explain what the test was or why it was being given to him. He gave Arturo two pencils and looked at his watch.

"Arthur, you must open this test and start when I say 'go,'" he said. "Do you understand? *Comprenday?*"

Arturo said, "Excuse me, *señor. Por favor*, do you speak Spanish . . . in case I need *ayuda*, some help with this?"

The man said, "Sorry, *no hablah espanyol*, and I am not allowed to help anyway." He looked down at the second hand on his watch and then said, "Go now." Then the man turned away.

Arturo opened the test paper and began answering. He had trouble reading many of the words and questions in the test. Many parts asked about things he did not understand, such as, "Who was Genghis Khan?" and "Why is it better to pay bills by check than cash," and "What color are rubies?"

The first half of the test was very hard. The second half was made up of numbers and puzzles and shapes. Arturo thought he did better on that.

Before Arturo could finish the last page, the man announced, "Time to stop."

Arturo was surprised. The man had not warned him that there was a time limit, and Arturo had no way to keep track of time anyway. The man picked up the test paper. "You can go out to play and then go home for today. Come back here tomorrow, and we will tell you what classroom you should go to."

When Arturo came back the next day, he was told to go to Classroom 15. He knew that was not where most of the other third graders were sitting. When he got to the new classroom, there were about a dozen children, all Mexican except for one Anglo boy off in a corner. The teacher was nice. She handed out coloring books and pencils. Day after day, the class was coloring, cutting out pictures, doing a little bit of very easy addition and subtraction and recess.

With Arturo were Diana, María, Manuel, Rachel, Ramón, Armando, Margarita and Ernesto. They ranged in age from seven to thirteen but were in the same classroom together all day. Diana, who with her twin brother Armando was the youngest, spoke hardly any English. She was absent on many days because, she told Arturo, "*Hay que ayudar en casa cuidando a los* babies *mientras mamá y papá trabajan.*" [I need to help at home to take care of the babies while my mother and father are working.] She asked Arturo to help her learn English, and he was glad to teach her as best he could.

Arturo asked María, "Why are we in this place instead of *real* school?"

María replied, "This is the room for kids they think are dummies. They never give us anything to do but baby stuff. I hate it."

A year later, Arturo was still in the same room. Other children on the playground both shunned and teased Diana, Arturo, María and the others, calling them "retard" and "*tonto*" and laughing at them.

Arturo, Diana and María didn't know it then but they were among the more than 13,000 Mexican-American children wrongfully placed in California's Educable Mentally Retarded (EMR) classes before 1979. And all of them had been relegated to these classes based on culturally biased IQ tests given in a language the children did not read or understand.(The term "retarded," now considered pejorative, has been dropped from use by professionals and others and replaced with terms such as "mentally impaired" or "intellectually disabled." But "retarded" and/or "EMR" were the terms used when the events in this book occured, they were part of the name-calling the affected children were subjected to and thus they are used herein to present an accurate picture of the times.)

The children in the class had complained to their parents, but the parents did not know what they could do. María's mother had gone to the school and asked, with the little English she knew, why the children were not learning more with the little English she knew. The teacher had smiled indulgently and said, "Don't worry. They are in a 'special class.' It will be fine and it is better here for them." No teacher, psychologist or anyone else from the school ever visited the labor camp to see how the children fared in their home environment.

The idea of mounting a legal challenge was completely foreign to the Soledad labor camp parents. They had no understanding of the justice system, did not know any attorneys or have the ability to afford them. While a small minority of Mexican-American school psychologists in California had railed against the use of biased IQ tests, the California Department of Education had blithely ignored them.

In 1964, Lyndon Johnson launched the "Great Society" and the "War on Poverty" initiative, which established social services, and included the creation of the national Legal Services Program. One of the programs initiated with Legal Services Program funds was California Rural Legal Assistance (CRLA). In late 1966, CRLA opened offices across rural California to provide legal representation for farmworkers and other rural low-income individuals. At that time, this was a revolutionary development.

In mid-1969, CRLA attorneys Marty Glick and Mo Jourdane became counsel for Diana, Arturo, María, and the other Soledad children. Eventually they came to represent the 13,000 children across California improperly labeled mentally retarded in a class action lawsuit, as well as at least 100,000 other such children who were on the threshold of a similar fate. Working with dedicated members of the Association of Chicano Psychologists, they filed a class action case known as *Diana v. State Board of Education* to challenge the use of English-only and culturally biased IQ tests to justify the placement and retention of the Mexican-American children in classes for the mentally retarded. The battle raged for a decade. This is the story of CRLA's and its early work in reversing the course of events for the Soledad Children.

—*Marty Glick and Mo Jourdane*

PART ONE
# 1964–1966
# BEGINNING AND ORGANIZING

# Chapter 1
## THE BIRTH OF THE LEGAL
## SERVICES PROGRAM

In the face of massive resistance from his southern colleagues, Lyndon Johnson successfully piloted into law the Civil Rights Act of 1964 and the Voting Rights Act of 1965. These were just the beginning as he turned next to his "Great Society" and ambitious "War on Poverty." Four different acts of Congress made up the foundation of Johnson's "War": The Social Security Act of 1965 (which established Medicare and Medicaid), the Food Stamp Act of 1964, The Elementary and Secondary Education Act and the Economic Opportunity Act of 1964.

The Office of Economic Opportunity (OEO) was the agency established to implement the Act of 1964. Former Peace Corps director Sargent Shriver was appointed on October 16, 1964 to be the first director of the OEO, which provided low-income individuals and families "opportunity" through access to better schooling, job training, decent housing and health and human services. The agency had the goal of helping poor people achieve "economic" self-sufficiency. Pioneer programs created by the OEO included Head Start, Job Corps, Upward Bound, Community Action and Vista.

The first two Presidents of the OEO, Clint Bamberger and Earl Johnson, Jr., recognized that a significant obstacle was the inability of recipients to enforce their right to the benefits offered by the new programs. There were no trained legal advocates to reform unfair and repressive policies and practices preventing equal opportunity for low-income clients.

In an influential article published in the *Yale Law Journal* in 1964, "The War on Poverty: A Civilian Perspective," authors Edgar and Jean Kahn made the case for the establishment of a nationwide network of independent, full-time civil lawyers. Traditional legal aid, usually managed by county bar associations, provided limited assistance to indigents, and individual private attorneys, especially in rural areas, lacked the resources to mount sustained and expensive litigation aimed at major issues or local businesses. As an example of the limited resources available, annual funds appropriated or otherwise raised in the mid-1960s for volunteer Los Angeles legal aid lawyers to serve that entire county totaled only $120,000.

To address this deficit, in 1966, the OEO Legal Services Program (LSP) was created to establish local offices across the nation staffed by attorneys whose practice would be devoted to representation of qualified low-income individuals. In a sense, these offices were to provide on the civil side the same sort of representation that public defenders provided to indigents accused of criminal misconduct. A critical advocate for the program's creation was the president of the American Bar Association (who would later become a United States Supreme Court justice), Lewis Powell. Powell, Sargent Shriver and other leaders insisted that the LSP be independent of local governments, state and local bar associations and local community action programs.

At the outset, LSP established client eligibility standards that placed ceilings on income earned and assets owned to qualify for free legal services to ensure that grantees would not compete with local bar members. The programs could not undertake cases seeking money damages nor could they take on fee-generating cases, such as contingency cases, unless they were able to show that the private bar had refused, after at least three referrals, to take on particular cases that could result in damages or fee awards.

In 1966, the OEO invited applications from organizations and groups interested in forming local law offices to carry out the mandates of the program. Between 1966 and 1971, 157 legal assistance programs were funded in 49 states with an appropriation that was initially $25 million and went up to $72 million by 1972.

Earl Johnson had taken over the OEO by 1967 and announced that dedication to "law reform" would be a top priority in OEO consideration of those applications. Neither the millions of previously unrepresented poor nor those routinely taking advantage of them had any idea what was on the horizon with the launch of these new programs.

| | |
|---|---|
| 1 | El Centro |
| 2 | Gilroy |
| 3 | Healdsburg /Santa Rosa |
| 4 | Madera |
| 5 | Marysville |
| 6 | McFarland |
| 7 | Modesto |
| 8 | Salinas |
| 9 | Santa Rosa |
| 10 | Sacramento |

Map of California showing CRLA offices

# Chapter 2
## JIM LORENZ AND CRLA

In Los Angeles in 1966, California Rural Legal Assistance's soon-to-be founder, James D. Lorenz, Jr., was just one of an army of young associate attorneys mostly assigned to legal research in the library of the very large O'Melveny & Myers firm. Born and raised in Dayton, Ohio, Jim graduated with honors from Harvard Law School and passed the 1965 bar exam. Jim was soon discontented with his work at the large commercial law firm. He later explained, "It is like running barefoot through wet sand and leaving no footprints. I needed to do something that would matter."

From Ohio, he had read about the plight of California farmworkers and the nascent attempts of César Chávez to start a union. To learn more, Jim visited several farm labor camps in Southern California and interviewed migrant workers and community group leaders. He read with interest about the new federal program and thought that farmworker legal services would make a critical difference. He spoke with César Chávez, Chicano political leader Bert Corona and several others to learn more about the history of migrant labor in California. Jim read the published OEO guidelines and put together a comprehensive grant application with the novel idea of creating a unified, statewide network of offices to provide services to California rural communities and farmworkers. Jim knew very well that local establishments in rural counties would resist a program that would bring attorneys with resources to challenge existing practices. He also recognized that an office in a small town like El Centro, California, staffed by what would often be inexperienced young attorneys, would need support from a central office in a major city, where senior attorneys could be available to both help with important litigation and combat efforts by powerful interests to undermine the program politically.

Jim's brief experience talking with farmworkers had taught him that the target client group for rural legal services would distrust law enforcement and a legal system they had only encountered in adverse situations. Therefore, the grant application specified that each office would have "community workers," an entirely new breed of paralegals from the communities they were serving, who could speak Spanish and explain to the clients that these lawyers were on their side. To accomplish all this, Jim proposed the establishment of California Rural Legal Assistance with nine offices in California's key agricultural valleys; each office would have two or three attorneys and two or more community workers. The central office would be in Los Angeles (the office moved to San Francisco in 1968).

The initial setup called for offices in (1) El Centro, in Imperial County, near the Mexican border; (2) McFarland, in Kern County, and near Delano where the United Farm Workers organization was headquartered; (3) Madera, just north of Fresno in the Central San Joaquin Valley; (4) Modesto, in the northern part of the Valley; (5) Marysville, in a rural area north of Sacramento; (6) Santa Rosa/Healdsburg, in the Sonoma County wine region; (7) Gilroy, now the self-proclaimed "Garlic Capital of the World" just south of San Jose; (8) Santa Maria, in Ventura County near Santa Barbara; (9) Salinas, in the center of a rich agricultural region that includes Monterey County.

Jim organized and registered California Rural Legal Assistance in early 1966. He submitted his *Proposal to Aid Farm Workers and Other Poor Persons Residing in the Rural Areas of California* to OEO Legal Services on May 24, 1966. The application concisely stated the problem CRLA would address:

> So far as the rural poor are concerned, the familiar saying that we are a society of laws, not of men, is, at best, a half-truth. Laws are passed, interpreted and enforced by men; legal

rights depend on political, economic and legal representation. Yet this is what the rural poor, particularly the farmworkers, have consistently lacked. Those who migrate from job to job are unable to comply with residency requirements which must be satisfied to vote and to receive welfare assistance, so that, by and large, they are unrepresented by the politician and unaided by the welfare worker. Some rural practitioners appear to be loath to give him legal assistance relating to wages, working conditions, and labor relations for fear such legal advice will only strengthen his economic bargaining position with the farmer and grower. In the words of the Senate Subcommittee on Migratory Labor, the plight of the farmworker is "shocking." He is the always excluded American.

Two months later, the OEO made its initial grant of $1,276,138 to establish the program. Jim's next task was to find and recruit dedicated attorneys to staff the diverse CRLA offices.

# Chapter 3
## MARTY GLICK

Marty Glick was among the first lawyers recruited by California Rural Legal Assistance. Marty was born and raised in Portsmouth, a small town in Southeast Ohio close to the Kentucky border. Marty's parents were descendants of families that had escaped the repressive regime of the Czars in Russia. Marty's maternal grandfather was smuggled out in a hay wagon. Louis Glick, Marty's father, was born in 1899 and raised as the youngest of six in Cleveland, Ohio, where the family operated a small grocery store. He had to drop out of high school to work in the family store during the Depression. Celia Genelin, born in London, England in 1913, was the youngest of five and moved with her family to Windsor, Ontario when she was a teenager. They eventually moved across Lake Erie to Detroit, where she completed her high school education. Both parents taught their children the importance of understanding cultural difference and freedom from discrimination as well as the virtues of hard work.

For his ninth birthday, his dad told Marty, "I have a special present for you. This is an important book written about a famous Jewish lawyer in New York named Samuel Lebowitz. Lebowitz tried many famous cases and overcame long odds for his clients." Marty eagerly unwrapped the present and found *Not Guilty*, written by Fred Pasley. It was the story of Lebowitz's renowned civil rights and criminal cases, including the infamous "Scottsboro Boys" murder case. The courtroom stories of social justice fascinated Marty, and he asked his dad for more books like that one.

His father told him about the exploits of Clarence Darrow and other famous advocates for civil rights and said, "I was sure you would like these stories because you argue with me and your mother incessantly. You would make a good lawyer." Thus, Marty had decided before he was ten he would become a trial lawyer and get involved in civil rights cases.

Marty attended The Ohio State University in Columbus and graduated with a B. A. in philosophy in 1961. At The Ohio State Law School he became Chief Justice of the Student Court (a student-run body that heard appeals from student disciplinary actions and traffic citations on campus) and graduated first in his OSU 1964 law school class.

The historic "1964 Mississippi Summer" marked the incursion into the South of an army of civil rights activists from the North, determined to assist African Americans in registering to vote. In 1964, three of these workers were murdered in Philadelphia, Mississippi. During his senior year in law school, Marty had sought and accepted a job with the Civil Rights Division of the United States Justice Department in Washington, DC. In July, Marty reported to work at the Justice Department, not far from the Capitol building. On his first day, after filling out some forms, he was ushered into the office of his immediate supervisor, D. Robert Owen. Decorating the walls of Owen's outer-office were individual maps of each of the 82 Mississippi counties. Owen assigned Marty to the Civil Rights Division, Southwest Section, and he was to spend significant parts of the next two years in the territory that covered Mississippi and Louisiana. There he worked with an elite Justice Department team headed by Owen and John Doar, a brilliant attorney and mentor to his young staff of lawyers. Doar was the first-ever top Civil Rights Division executive to travel extensively throughout Mississippi, Alabama, Louisiana, Tennessee, Georgia and other southern states. He visited the rural areas and the cities in the South, talking to leaders of all races, seeking to understand the issues on the ground. Doar went to Alabama in 1961 to organize protection for the Freedom Riders. In 1962, he stood with James Meredith, resisting George Wallace's attempts to prevent Meredith from entering the University of Mississippi at Oxford. In March 1965, he marched with Martin Luther King the 54 miles from Selma to Montgomery, Alabama, organizing protection and support and encouraging the powerful non-violent protest that the march conveyed. Most famously, on June 15, 1963, after the funeral in Jackson, Mississippi of assassinated NAACP Field Secretary Medgar Evers, when angry mourners armed with rocks were confronted by squadrons of police armed with rifles and wearing riot gear, Doar stepped off the sidewalk and into the middle of the street between the antagonistic forces and shouted, "My name is John Doar . . . D-O-A-R. I'm from the Justice Department, and everyone around here knows I stand for what is right." Turning to the protesters, he said, "You can't win with bricks and bottles. Medgar Evers wouldn't want it this way." Slowly, the marchers complied.

Decades later, when Marty and his Civil Rights division colleague Gene Livingston had breakfast with John before he was to be honored at the Kennedy Center, they asked John what moved him to spell out his name at that moment. John replied, "I was used to spelling out my name when I am asked for it so they don't think it is D-O-O-R. It was all I could think of to do when I found myself in the street between the rocks and the guns when I knew I had to say something."

Marty's first assignment, working with John Doar, Bob Owen and others in the division, was the investigation and prosecution of the killers of the three civil rights workers, Michael Schwerner, James Chaney and Andrew Goodman, murdered by Klansmen in Philadelphia, Mississippi. Marty was part of a platoon of young Justice Department attorneys who flew to Jackson in July 1964 and took up headquarters in Meridian in Lauderdale County, just southeast of Neshoba County. By day, they drove by the oak and pine forests in the clay hills and bottom lands and numerous creeks of Southeast Mississippi to the small, highly segregated Mississippi town of Philadelphia and worked there with several dozen FBI agents assigned from throughout the South. They interviewed residents of the "Negro Quarter" who had been victims of beatings and other forms of intimidation in Neshoba County. They asked those who could and would identify perpetrators to testify at on-going grand jury proceedings in Biloxi. Despite the secrecy of the grand jury, black residents of Philadelphia were frightened and skeptical that their identities would be protected.

One elderly man said to Marty, "Good you are here now, but soon you will go home to your nice home in the North, but I will still be here with these Klan police. Why should I go talk to some grand jury?"

Marty responded, "I understand, but if you and others don't act, then what will happen is that thirty-some years from now, my son will be here asking your son to be the one to step forward, because nothing will have changed."

The man thought for a few moments and then said, "Okay, I'll be going on down to Biloxi. See you there."

As depicted in the movie, *Mississippi Burning*, relationships between the FBI and the local Philadelphia, Mississippi police in the summer of 1964 were tense and deeply antagonistic. On one occasion, Marty received orders from the team working in Biloxi to serve a subpoena on a man named Jordan who was the head of Philadelphia's "Auxiliary Police," which they believed to be a pseudonym for the Klan. Marty thought it might be prudent to have an FBI agent along when he served Mr. Jordan at his home. He stopped by the small motel room that was serving as FBI headquarters in Philadelphia where they were cooped up. It was far too small to contain the agents and their increasingly fraying nerves. It seemed to Marty that the FBI there, imported from all over the South and Midwest to engage in the hunt for the missing civil rights workers, were constantly disassembling, reassembling and cleaning their weapons in anticipation of a fight, and they were unabashed in expressing their dislike and disdain for the local "redneck" sheriff and deputies.

"I need to serve a subpoena on the auxiliary police guy Jordan. Anyone have time to come along?" Marty asked.

At least a dozen jumped up to volunteer, but one nicknamed "Flash" Gordon was quickest to act. "I'm a-comin' with you, no way I miss this."

Gordon and another agent drove Marty in their FBI Ford rental to Jordan's two-bedroom house on a tree-lined street in the whitest part of town. They parked in a shadow-covered spot across the street and one house down from the Jordan residence.

Flash said, "Marty, after you serve him, he's gonna hit you . . . and when he does, duck real hard and quick to the right."

"Why do that?"

"'Cause as soon as he hits you, I'ma gonna drill 'im." And, without waiting for a response, Flash and the other agent moved back alongside their parked Ford.

Marty went up onto the porch and rang the bell while the two agents in their tan FBI-issue raincoats tried to look unobtrusive standing under a tree on the other side of the road. He was more concerned about Flash behind him than Jordan in the house. Mrs. Jordan answered the door.

"My husband's here but jest finishin' up takin' his bath. You kin come on in and wait if you like," she said hospitably, gesturing for Marty to go inside.

Marty said, "Thanks very much, Mrs. Jordan, but it's a nice day and so I'll just wait out here on the porch."

"Suit yourself. I'll send him on out when he's done."

As time passed with no action, Flash, trying to keep a low profile, sidled across the street and whispered, "What the heck is he doing?"

Marty replied, "Taking a bath."

Flash nodded skeptically and retreated to his post.

Five minutes later, a fresh soap-smelling Jordan opened the door and accepted his subpoena to be at the grand jury in Biloxi the next day with a smile and a thank you and no punch.

When Marty and his fellow Civil Rights Division attorneys arrived in Philadelphia in July 1964, Schwerner, Chaney and Goodman were still missing. Police records showed that Deputy Sheriff Cecil Price had arrested them in the afternoon of June 21,

1964, and released them that evening. They were never seen again. The local Mississippi newspapers quoted Mississippi Governor Paul Johnson, Jr. stating, "[They're] just fine and hiding out with Fidel Castro in Cuba." Johnson made no comment when the FBI found the boys' burned-out station wagon abandoned in a remote area on June 29. Based on the report of a similar prior arrest, release and recapture of a local, black college student named Wilmer Faye Jones, the FBI suspected that the Deputy Sheriff had released but then later stopped the three civil rights workers on the highway and turned them over to local Ku Klux Klan members riding in a green pickup truck. They believed the Klan members had then assassinated the trio and disposed of their bodies as a lesson to other northerners who might think of interfering in their racist domain.

The Civil Rights Division attorneys working in Philadelphia were warned by the FBI to be out of the county by sunset and were always to travel in twos and check in with the FBI twice a day. As time went on and the demands of the work intensified, they stopped diligently checking in and leaving at sunset. One moonlit evening in late July, Marty and his Civil Rights Division colleague Terry Lenzner had been working late in Neshoba County. At about nine that night, with Marty driving, and both Terry and Marty still wearing their required suits and ties, they were on the highway headed back to the Justice Department headquarters in Meridian. Ten minutes into the journey, a patrol car suddenly appeared behind them and turned on its red flashing light. Marty slowed and found a spot to pull over. As he did so, he saw a green pickup truck with a group of men sitting in the bed pull over opposite them. The driver let it idle.

The patrolman was abrupt and hostile. "Let me see your driver's license and identification right now."

When Marty complied, the burly officer said, "Who are you and just what are you doing in my county at this time of night?"

Marty said, "Sir, we are attorneys working with the United States Department of Justice on assignment."

"Show me your ID," was the next demand.

Neither Terry nor Marty had official credentials because pro-
cessing them was a six-week project for the Justice Department.
All they had to give to the patrolman was their Justice Department
building passes.

With a sneer, the officer said, "This all you have?"

Marty explained that they were new and asked the patrol officer, "What did you stop us for, sir?"

He raised his voice: "You were weaving, constantly crossing
over the yellow line in the middle of the road, like there was something wrong with you and you were drunk."

Marty knew he had been driving with care but also that on the
curvy, narrow country road back to Meridian, it was almost impossible not to occasionally cross the center line. Talking back seemed
like a poor option, so he stayed silent.

The patrolman glared at Lenzner and growled, "When I got
out of my car, you dropped your hands to your waist. Why did
you do that? Do you have a weapon?" (All the while, the idling
green pickup with the group of men in it had not moved.)

Marty cringed when he heard Terry's response, "I'm from New
York. In New York, the highway patrol wants us to get out of the
car when stopped, so I was just reaching down to undo my seat-
belt."

The over-sized officer drew himself up and shouted, "Well,
you're not in New York, now, boy. You're in the great state of Mississippi and you will do things our way here, boy. Do you understand me clearly?"

Terry murmured, "Yes, sir, I do."

The patrolman regarded them closely, no doubt noticing their
dress clothes were nothing like what the civil rights activists wore.
After a long pause, he seemed to gesture towards the green pickup, and it drove off.

He said, "I'll let you-all off this time with a warning and expect
not to be seeing you anywhere 'round here ever again."

The young lawyers were very happy to get back to Meridian
that evening. They returned to Philadelphia the next day and in
the days that followed. August 4, 1964, on a hot and sultry day,

and acting on information from an "unidentified" source, the FBI invited the press to join them as they dug into an earthen dam on the Old Jolly Farm owned by Olan Burrage, one of nineteen co-conspirators in the crime. There they uncovered the bodies of the three murdered civil rights activists. Seven of the nineteen, later indicted on federal charges, including the Deputy Sheriff, were prosecuted by John Doar for the United States and convicted in 1967, and an eighth, Edgar Ray "Preacher" Killen, was convicted of manslaughter by a Mississippi state court jury forty-one years later.

The work for the Civil Rights Division was intense as the attorneys made frequent trips on the narrow two-lane roads of Mississippi and Louisiana, working very long days and nights. Marty worked on a variety of cases that concerned voting rights, public accommodation and other civil and criminal litigation. Cases he worked on included the murder of Hattiesburg civil rights leader Vernon Dahmer, the desegregation of Primo's Restaurant in Jackson, a contempt action against Voter Registrar Theron Lynd, who had systematically discriminated against African American applicants, and an action before a three-judge court in New Orleans that resulted in an injunction against some eighty members of the Bogalusa, Louisiana, Ku Klux Klan. Marty also argued to a three-judge court in New Orleans, defending the constitutionality of the Voting Rights Act and, on a Primary Election Day in 1966, stood with Charles Evers and United States Marshals in Fayette, Mississippi, protecting African Americans who went to the polls to vote.

One night in July 1966, Marty received a phone call from Bob Gnaizda, a friend of his Los Angeles internship days.

"Total change of plans," Gnaizda exclaimed. "Instead of me going to DC to work, you need to get ready *at once* to come to California."

"What are you talking about?" Marty asked.

Bob replied, "I met this attorney a couple of days ago . . . Jim Lorenz. He's heading up a new program out here named 'California Rural Legal Assistance.' It is perfect for us. . . . We'll have complete control. But you gotta get here to LA in a week in order to establish residency to qualify for the next bar exam. You need to move your butt, like right now. I'm already signed up. I'll be assigned to the Salinas office."

"Where the heck is that?"

"Don't worry about it! But I told Lorenz that I'd only sign if he hired you, too."

"What the . . . "

"And he agreed to take you . . . sight unseen, kiddo!"

Bob was talking so fast Marty could hardly get a word in edgewise. Bob touted the benefits of the job, both living in Monterey County and the opportunity to be a legal services pioneer for farmworkers and other rural poor. Then, slowing down and lowering his voice to a whisper, Bob said, "We can even take on and abolish the Bracero Program."

Marty had no idea what a *bracero* was or why Gnaizda was whispering, but he was too embarrassed to ask.

"Bob, slow down. There's just no way I'm going to LA inside of one week. I need to talk to Jim Lorenz first, read about this new program and then discuss the whole thing with my wife. And I have to make sure I'm not leaving the Division without finishing up the cases I am working on."

Bob, nevertheless, was insistent and persuasive about what CRLA could be, and a few weeks later, Marty accepted the offer. In November 1966, Marty arrived in Los Angeles and began working in the CRLA Central Office while studying for and then taking the 1967 California bar exam. Days after the exam, Marty moved to Monterey County and joined the CRLA Salinas office to work for the program there, as planned.

# Chapter 4
## CRLA OPENS FOR CLIENTS

Remarkably, the California State Bar formally opposed the grant to create CRLA. Lorenz had sent a copy of the CRLA grant application to the board of governors of the state bar. "That shows how green and naïve I was, because I expected them to give me an award since I was going to do all these wonderful things for farmworkers," Jim later recounted. Instead, the state bar board of governors unanimously passed a resolution in April 1966, urging that CRLA either not be funded at all or abandon its plan to provide what the state bar labeled "militant advocacy for one side of an economic struggle (the union seeking to represent farmworkers)." The director of the OEO, Sargent Shriver, told the state bar president that "if the state bar would agree that none of its members will represent growers, I will agree that no legal services program lawyers will represent the pickers." Of course, the state bar would or could do no such thing.

After a series of negotiations between the California bar leadership, the OEO and Lorenz, in June 1967, the parties signed an "Agreement of Understanding." Their truce provided that a majority of the CRLA board of directors would always be attorneys, that the state bar would appoint two members to the CRLA board, and each local bar where CRLA had an office would also appoint one representative. While CRLA could not represent the United Farm Worker Union, it could represent individual farmworkers.

The first CRLA office opened was in Madera, a small country township thirty miles north of Fresno near the geographic center of California in the huge San Joaquin Valley. Modesto, about an hour north of Madera, was scheduled to open in the fall of 1966. The Stanislaus County Bar Association filed a lawsuit to enjoin the office from operating and, in October 1966, a local Superior Court judge granted a temporary restraining order delaying the opening. Ten days later, when the Stanislaus Association was unable to offer anything more than its unsubstantiated fears that the CRLA would encourage "radical and unethical behavior;" the injunction was lifted, the case dismissed and the doors opened. The other seven offices were also operating by the end of 1966.

The core group of staff members had experience in law firms large and small as well as in the legal departments of federal and state agencies. CRLA hired attorneys whose specialization and experience covered a vast array of services. What it did lack, however, was ethnic and gender diversity—par for the course at that time in history. In the mid-1960s, there were few Hispanic attorneys in the California bar and an even smaller number were ready to trust their careers to a new and untested program. However, Jim did convince an experienced thirty-six-year-old, Armando Rodríguez, to head up the Madera office. His younger brother Rubén joined CRLA as a community worker. Carol Ruth Silver and Trudy Chern were hired to be lead lawyers in McFarland and Santa Maria.

CRLA paused at the outset to determine what issues were most vital to its farmworkers and other clients in order to launch an in-depth plan to specialize. After substantial investigation, including meetings with local community-based organizations, elected leaders, other legal services programs and bar associations, among others, CRLA determined to create four impact groups it called task forces. Included initially, alongside Housing, Employment and Public Benefits was the Education Task Force. Its mandate was to consider the issues of enrollment, equal opportunity, bilingual services, progression, discipline, discrimination, teacher quality, parent involvement and school funding. As with the other groups, the Education Task Force went to work at the outset by researching laws, regulations and publications about education issues affecting particularly the rural poor and farmworkers. The task force members met periodically to make assignments, receive reports, study published statistics and identify priorities for issues that adversely affected large numbers of clients. The Education Task Force's first leader and its chairperson for the first six years was Marty Glick in Salinas.

PART TWO
# 1966–1969
# THE SALINAS OFFICE

# CHAPTER 5
## THE SALINAS CRLA OFFICE

In 1967, Salinas was a beautiful town with good weather, tree-lined streets and surrounded by rows of lettuce, tomatoes, berries, broccoli and other crops in the fields as far as the eye could see. It was headquarters for many of the largest and most successful California agricultural companies. Highway 101 bisects Salinas; the longest continuous highway in California, Highway 101 is 808 miles long and stretches in the North past majestic redwood trees to the Oregon bor-

| | | | |
|---|---|---|---|
| 1. | Prunedale | 7. | King City |
| 2. | Salinas | 8. | Castroville |
| 3. | Chualar | 9. | Monterey |
| 4. | Gonzales | 10. | Pebble Beach |
| 5. | Soledad | 11. | Carmel |
| 6. | Greenfield | 12. | Big Sur |

der; it is also the major artery connecting San Francisco with Los Angeles.

The Salinas office was on Main Street in the heart of downtown. The office was furnished with an old wooden reception desk, a second-hand Naugahyde couch and randomly placed folding chairs resting on a linoleum-covered cement floor. On a corner coffee table sat a single-bulb lamp with pamphlets in English and Spanish for "How to Apply for Public Assistance," "How to Handle Your Own Case in Small Claims Court" and "How You Can Live on a Budget." Each of the attorney offices had a second-hand desk, an old wooden chair and a bookshelf. A 9'x12' storage room in the back served as the library with a limited set of law books donated by a retiring local attorney. To really do legal research, the lawyers had to visit the law library on the second floor of the courthouse a half a mile away.

Josephine Rohr had attended law school in Puerto Rico. She was head legal secretary and sometimes investigator for the office. Josephine knew as much or more immigration law than any licensed attorney in Salinas. A second legal secretary was Amelia Harris, the Latina wife of a Salinas fireman. Angie Valenzuela was the welcoming receptionist. Angie, Amelia, and Josephine were all bilingual and each brought her own experiences from the communities in and around Salinas to the office. Thus, they were important participants in discussions about issues and priorities.

The first attorney hired to work in Salinas was Notre Dame Law School graduate Dennis Powell. Denny, recruited by Jim Lorenz from the Department of Treasury in Virginia, soon transferred to the Madera CRLA office. As directing attorney of that office, he won a California Supreme Court case granting an injunction against a local school district that had cancelled classes and required first graders and other Mexican-American school children to instead work in the fields harvesting grapes.

One of the original community workers in Salinas was the 68-year-old Tony Del Bueno, a veteran of the Mexican Revolution. Tony spoke Spanish and Sicilian fluently and was a certified interpreter in both languages. Despite his limited formal education, Tony was passionately devoted to CRLA's education issues. He was also a frequent motivational speaker at state agencies and colleges in the area as well as for a variety of community groups. After two years working with the Salinas office, Tony transferred to Gilroy, where he worked well into his seventies.

Ladislao Pineda and José Pérez were the other original community workers attached to the Salinas Office. Also bilingual, they came from families with farmworker backgrounds. José was a Salinas native and Ladislao had grown up as a farmworker in Visalia before joining the Navy. Both were smart high school graduates, enthusiastic about the new advocacy CRLA was providing for its clients in the community.

José, very early on, brought in to Marty what the farmworker community called "*el cortito*," a hoe required by California growers. It was short-handled, only 8- to 12-inches long, and therefore only useful for weeding when the farmworker stooped over with their back bent. José said, "Marty, if you want to really do something for farmworkers, you need to attack this thing and get it thrown away. It is killing the workers." José hung it on the wall in Marty's office as a reminder, but several years would pass before Mo Jourdane and Marty would come up with and implement a plan of action to get the short hoe banned.

In January 1969, Enrique ("Henry") Cantú joined the CRLA Salinas staff. Henry was born in Mexico, then came to the United States as part of a farmworker family and grew up in Sanger, near Fresno. He had been selected by the Mayor of Sanger to receive training in Washington, DC, to qualify as an adult teacher for the Central California Action Associates. Henry was later quoted in the CRLA monthly newsletter as saying, "I go straight to the people, go to their houses, eat where they eat and so on. That is how you really know what their needs really are." Henry was himself a victim of the mislabeling of farmworker children as "retarded." He would later provide important testimony in California legislative hearings connected to the Diana case.

Another community worker, Hector de la Rosa, would become the critical conduit between the parents of Arturo and the other children stuck in the Soledad EMR class and CRLA. Hector was born in Aguascalientes City in central Mexico. At the age of six,

Hector moved with his parents to Ciudad Juárez, where his family became involved in moving produce from El Paso across the border and reselling it to consumers in Juárez for a nice profit. Hector's mother Socorro would help package the produce for sale. She also worked as a dishwasher. When not in school, Hector would play in the kitchens where his mother washed dishes.

Hector often told the story of how his father " . . . dug this hole in the ground under the floor where we lived to put money away so that the family could migrate to the United States." The De la Rosas finally got their break when Socorro was able to use a friend's green card and a borrowed birth certificate for young Hector—and they had to pay a *coyote* $400.

When the family settled into a shack in rural New Mexico, Hector was able to start school: "After a few months, it felt safe, so we moved to a small house in Atoka, a tiny community near Artesia, and my parents insisted that I go to the school to get an education." Hector spoke no English at all. "The math I learned in Juárez served me well enough in school in Artesia, because I didn't need to know English to figure out the numbers, but I was really struggling in my other classes because I couldn't understand. Then I made friends with the other brown face in our class, a boy named Daniel. Daniel spoke English and Spanish, and we would talk quietly on the playground as he was helping me with my English. One time, the teacher caught us speaking Spanish, a forbidden practice, and we were marched in to see the school principal, Mr. Ford. The teacher kept repeating to us one of the few phrases in Spanish she even knew, '*chicos mucho malo*.'"

Apparently, either this "No Spanish policy" was because the school authorities were suspicious of what the kids were saying or because they believed that a child will be forced, if deprived entirely of Spanish, to learn English by some sort of osmosis. Mr. Ford told the boys to be discrete but it was okay for Daniel to help Hector learn English.

Then one day, there was a knock on the door of the family's small rural home. "There was a Border Patrol agent at the door when we opened it. He had a hat, badge and belt like Smokey the Bear."

The agent asked for their papers, and when they were not forthcoming, he told Hector's parents, "The law requires you and your family to leave the country."

Hector's father Leo pointed to Socorro and her obvious condition. "My wife is due to have our baby any day now and if she goes into labor during our trip back to Juarez it could be very bad. Can't you help us?"

The agent was sympathetic. He said, "Okay, it looks to me like you have a US citizen coming there. I'm going to give you some papers to fill out. I'll be back here in six months, and if you have your child and the papers are filled out, I'll get them processed so you can stay in the United States. From the looks of it, you've been a hard worker and law-abiding."

Hector's brother, Leopoldo, was born on March 14, 1950. Six months to the day later, the Border Patrol agent was back. He was glad to see young Leopoldo was healthy and he asked, "Have you completed the papers I left with you?"

Shaking his head, Leo replied, "You have been very kind, but my wife and I have decided it is too expensive for us to live in your country, especially with another mouth to feed. When the season changes and there is no work, it is very difficult. We have decided to return to Mexico, but thank you for helping us." The De la Rosa family moved to Torreón, a good-sized city in the state of Coahuila.

Hector was almost 13 by then. His public school education since first grade had been in English with no classes in Spanish language or grammar.

The principal in the Torreón school told Hector, "We need to figure out where to put you."

Hector protested. "What do you mean? I don't want to go backwards. I have done well in school in the United States."

The principal was unmoved and gave Hector books in Spanish to read out loud to him. Hector recalled, "I aced the first-grade *Julio and Juliano* (Jack and Jill) story, but I was stumped by the third-grade book. So the principal said he was putting me in the third grade. When I reported to the grade three classroom, I could hear very curious eight-year-olds wondering why this big guy was in their classroom." Hector advanced a full grade each half year until it was time for secondary school. He spent the next two years at the Academia Zaragoza learning public accounting.

In 1958, Hector's father received a call from José Torres: "Our Atoka farm is expanding and doing very well, and we could use your help. There is a new law in the United States, so I can now help you receive green cards for you and your family. You will all be legal, and I can pay you well."

Hector was not happy to hear the family would be moving again, but his father was the boss. A few months later, after they had received their promised official green cards, the family emigrated to New Mexico again; however, by the time the De la Rosa family arrived in Atoka, Torres was no longer in charge of the farm and there were no jobs. The family had no recourse but to do migrant farm work for the next two years, traveling from Texas to Arizona, California, Oregon, Washington, Idaho and Minnesota.

One evening, an El Paso neighbor informed Socorro that there were good opportunities for farmworkers near Oakland, California, and soon the De la Rosa family loaded up their 1942 Chevrolet and headed for Oakland. Passing through Soledad on the way, Leo announced, "This looks like a very good place to live. Maybe I should stop and see if there is any work."

Socorro shook her head, "We can always come back. Let's stick with the plan."

They continued on to Oakland, where it turned out that the farm work had become limited. Hector found temporary work cleaning out bathrooms in a movie theatre. Leo said they should go back to Soledad and see if there was work there. Once again, they packed up and headed back south and found work in the fields of Greenfield, just south of Soledad. The labor camp in Greenfield was for single men only, and the family was evicted when the effort to hide Socorro the first night failed. So they drove back up to Soledad, to the farm labor camp there. It was the camp mentioned earlier that had been originally built for World War II German prisoners.

The following day, Hector and his father went to the nearby lettuce fields and found steady work. The family decided to remain in the Soledad labor camp at least through the harvest. Hector met his wife María at the Catholic Church in Soledad, where they both sang in the choir. They soon married and, to earn a living, both migrated with the harvests in the western states for the next two years. After temporarily living in labor camps in Idaho and Washington, María told Hector, "I will migrate no more. We need to settle down where we can have a home and family."

They returned to the Soledad family camp, and Hector found work sweeping the floor and doing janitorial duties for Westcott Chevrolet, the only new car dealership in that town. After a stint as attendant at the attached Westcott service station, Hector advanced to apprentice auto mechanic.

It was here, one day in the Fall of 1966 that two representatives from CRLA found Hector and recruited him to the cause, after the local priest had recommended him to them. CRLA was to use the parish on Mondays to see clients, where Hector would serve as a translator and the local community expert. Hector kept his day job as a mechanic at first, and only worked part-time one evening a week. In October 1968, Hector began working full-time for CRLA. Fifty years later at age 77, Hector is still helping clients in Soledad, working for CRLA as its longest-serving employee anywhere in the program.

# Chapter 6
## EARLY SALINAS DAYS

Bob Gnaizda, the first CRLA directing attorney in Salinas, had more original and creative ideas in one day than anyone else would in a year. He would rattle them off in rapid order. Nine out of ten were either crazy or wildly impractical, usually both. But the tenth would be brilliant. Marty was a confident translator of Bob's best ideas into action; the pair were a force. They decided to accept new clients three days a week and carry a caseload of no more than forty active cases each so that their work would be thorough and effective. They could use the other two days and weekends to do the research and hard work required to win their high-impact cases.

After the office in Salinas opened, word spread that real lawyers were available, but it took some time for that message to reach the farmworker community. The CRLA Salinas office worked with community-based organizations and established a local advisory committee to provide input and to assist with out-reach to eligible clients. One evening every week, Bob and Tony Del Buono would hold office hours in Hollister to the north in San Benito County. On Monday evenings from five to seven or eight, Marty would join Hector in Soledad in the church parish hall to see clients there and enjoy a dinner of tamales or enchiladas prepared by María.

The change in the balance of power in Salinas and in Monterey county (and in the other CRLA office areas) upon the arrival of CRLA was palpable. Workers, tenants, abused wives, applicants for unemployment insurance and medical benefits, minority students and others without means had previously lacked the ability to fight against injustice. Abuses against individual's rights in minority and low-income communities had been rampant. Least protected of all were migrant workers and farm labor camp residents. The American justice system was built upon access to the courts, and those who couldn't afford to hire advocates to fight for them were reluctant to complain, lest their situation become even worse. They knew complaining would not accomplish anything.

In 1967, that changed because when these individuals were treated wrongly, they could be represented by dedicated and able lawyers who did not charge by the hour. The CRLA lawyers were willing to litigate and demand real remedies for the poor against those with power and means, be they large agribusinesses, collection agencies, elected officials or government agencies. Those who had held all the cards before CRLA came on the scene had to decide if they were still willing to pay their lawyers to pursue cases when their legal position was, at best, questionable. In many early instances, CRLA had but to articulate the challenge and the defendant folded.

None of this was lost on the Salinas members of the Monterey County bar. One early and outspoken CRLA opponent, a Salinas attorney named Bill Moreno, was particularly hostile. Moreno had given generously of his time to help indigents with service cases and had become known for his work with community charitable organizations. He told Gnaizda that he would fight CRLA every step of the way. "You could be on your death bed and ask me for a three-day extension," Moreno said, "and you won't get it."

In February 1967, Salinas bar members decided to convene a "special meeting" to discuss CRLA and what they might do to "deal with it." As a formality, Bob was invited to be on the panel at the event with seven other local lawyers. To the surprise of the bar members, Bob accepted immediately. Marty and Bob spent a few hours together preparing for Bob's remarks and likely responses. Most of the local bar members attended. Before the panel discussion started, Moreno, not invited to be up front, stood up and railed at each of the members of the panel. "I am the only one in this room who helps indigents regularly, and so none of you should be up there saying anything whatsoever," Moreno barked.

Moreno's blistering attack had the unintended effect of confirming that free legal services were needed in the county. In short, calm statements, Bob assured everyone that CRLA lawyers would work professionally with local bar members. The meeting concluded without any action being taken against CRLA. Marty and Bob's next encounter with attorney Moreno would have a very different tone.

# Chapter 7
## THE SALINAS STRAWBERRIES CASE

The parents of the children relegated to the class for the Educable Mentally Retarded who came to CRLA for help in 1969 might never have done so if CRLA had not rapidly made a name for itself as a fearless and effective advocate for farmworker families. In Salinas, that reputation began with the high profile Salinas Strawberries case.

At the time CRLA began its operations in Salinas, the grower community was deeply concerned about the perceived threat to the status quo posed by the soft-spoken but "vicious" César Chávez, the feisty and "outrageous" Dolores Huerta and the United Farm Workers Union. The union was not yet active in the Salinas Valley, but rumors of efforts to organize the 60,000 Hispanics working there were rampant. Particularly vigilant were the two prominent grower organizations in the area, the Growers Farm Labor Association and the Grower-Shipper Vegetable Association. Grower-Shipper was led by E. James Houseberg and his cohorts; they made it known that they wanted to hear immediately of any organizing attempts, which would be regarded as a virtual invasion. They put into effect plans to aggressively stamp out the threat and punish workers who had the audacity to join the Farm Workers Union.

Salinas Strawberries was a major berry company in the valley at the time. It employed 4,000 to 5,000 workers during peak harvest season, retaining approximately 125 of their most highly skilled and valued workers year-round. Included in the year-round group in 1967 were:

| NAME | AGE | POSITION | YEARS WITH COMPANY | CHILDREN |
|------|-----|----------|--------------------|----------|
| José Vázquez | 45 | Irrigator | 7 | 5 |
| Jesús Jaramillo | 33 | Irrigator and Driver | 6 | 8 |
| Rafael García | 28 | Crew Leader | 6 | 6 |
| Gilberto Hinojosa | 44 | Irrigator | 6 | 4 |
| Alvaro Hinojosa | 33 | Irrigator | 6 | 3 |

Also working for the company were four seasonally employed irrigators; three more Hinojosa brothers and a man named Wenceslao Salazar. Together with the five-year-round group, they were called "The Nine Strawberry Workers." A labor contractor named José Silva employed two other irrigators sent to work at the ranch at the time. In April of 1967, each of these workers were among the 60 farmworkers at Salinas Strawberries' Wing Nut Ranch near Chualar, 10 miles Southeast of Salinas.

On April 11, both Salinas Strawberries and José Silva received at their headquarter offices anonymous one-page letters in Spanish, accusing The Nine Strawberry Workers and the two men working with Silva of "going around making propaganda so that we join the union" and "we make a strike." The letter was supposedly from "Families of Waco Camp." Neither Salinas Strawberries nor Silva bothered to conduct any investigation into the allegations in the unsigned letters they received nor ask any of their long-time and previously trusted employees if the accusations were true. Instead, they decided to teach their entire workforce (and, indeed, all of the workers in the Salinas Valley) a dramatic lesson.

Two days later, on April 13, 1967 at 11 a.m., a Salinas Strawberries senior supervisor stopped work in the Chualar fields and assembled together all of their 60 employees. As the complaint later filed in court recited, "In front of this whole group, the names of the nine Strawberry workers were called out—one by one—and it was announced that each was fired." Each was escorted off the property by a physically imposing group of supervisors, who told them, " . . . not to be seen around Salinas Strawberries property ever again." The labor contractor also fired his two employees the same day, as demanded by Salinas Strawberries.

Not only were the men fired, but heat, water and electricity were turned off in their trailers in the employer-owned La Posada trailer camp. These men had many young children. The distressed and frightened families were threatened with forcible eviction if they refused the orders to pack up and leave within three days. The workers found their way to the CRLA office, where community worker José Pérez listened to their story and brought them to see Marty directly. José translated what had happened to the distraught families. The workers related that, in fact, only one of them had actually joined the Chávez union, and that individual had not told anyone or engaged in any organizing at all.

The California Labor Code had an explicit section, Section 923, prohibiting discharge of employees for exercising their free speech rights and their right to associate, but there was no precedent at the time for use of the labor code to protect farmworkers. No such case had ever been brought. The National Labor Relations Act did not apply at all, because farm work was an explicit exception to the coverage that protected almost all other workers.

Marty, not yet admitted to the California bar—the examination results would be in within a month or two—told Bob about the situation. "We know," Marty began, "that, notwithstanding the public and explicit 'union' firing of these workers, Salinas Strawberries will lie and deny that the workers were fired for supporting the union. The remaining employees will be too intimidated to get involved. I think we can use Section 923, but there is no precedent for it. So we'll need to make new law. What do you think about me calling over to Salinas Strawberries and trying to tell them that these guys were never union members? Maybe I can learn something."

Bob said, "Do it."

So, Marty called over to a Salinas Strawberries executive, who promptly challenged Marty's assertion that the workers were innocent of union activity. The arrogant executive was convinced Salinas Strawberries was bulletproof and allowed Marty access to review the files of the discharged employees. "Come on over, but you won't find a thing, and you're wasting your time and ours."

Later that day at the Salinas Strawberries office, the executive explained with a smirk on his face to Marty and Josephine Rohr that the workers were just laid off. "We have lots of turnover. Your new lawyers don't understand our agriculture business in any way. And, by the way, I haven't heard anything about these guys trying to organize a union."

The executive led them to a records room and pointed to a box containing the slim personnel records of the nine employees. "You can look through them, but there are just names and pay and hours worked. All you'll see is that we always paid as required. You be quick and then get the hell out."

A bored secretary, tasked with keeping an eye on Marty and Jo, was stationed across the room from the table where the boxed files were set up to be reviewed. She had brought a magazine in with her and ignored the CRLA visitors entirely.

Marty took the files out of the box and handed them to Jo. He then noticed in the back of the box, laying on its side, an unlabeled folder closed only with a large black binder clip. Unclipping and opening the unsealed folder, he was stunned to find nine sheets of paper, each with the individual names of the nine CRLA clients neatly typed at the top. Halfway down each of the pages was a statement in blue ink handwriting: *Fired for union member.* At the bottom of each was a signature that Marty presumed had been made by a personnel employee with the responsibility to record reasons for discharge. Also in the clipped folder were copies of the accusatory, anonymous letters in Spanish to the company and to José Silva.

Marty had no doubt that he would never see these records or the letters again if he left without them. He quietly passed them over to Josephine, who was equally astonished to see these smoking-gun documents.

Josephine whispered, "How are we going to get this incredible stuff out of this place?"

There were no cellphones in those days and they had no camera with them. There was, however, a Xerox copier in the room.

Marty whispered back, "Just be ready to copy."

Marty walked casually over to the secretary and asked, "Is it okay if we just Xerox copies of the employee files," he asked, holding them up without the anonymous letters which he'd put back in the box. "Then, we can get out of your way."

"I suppose so, but let me check first with my boss." She took the folders out to her boss, then came back and said, "He says you're okay to copy the records."

Marty handed the records to Jo and chatted with the secretary, letting her know that he and his wife were new to Monterey County and asking about her favorite restaurants and movie theatres. Meanwhile, Jo copied the entire contents of the box, including the sheets that stated, "Fired for union member."

Armed with the telling documents, CRLA filed suit against Salinas Strawberries and included the documents as exhibits. Superior Court Judge Gordon Campbell granted the workers' request for immediate relief precluding eviction and any continuing failure to provide utilities to the families in the camp. Notwithstanding all of the evidence CRLA had put together and the documents found in the box, Salinas Strawberries fought the case through discovery, taking depositions of the nine workers and the Silva men. The company filed motions contending that the labor code could not supplant farmworker exclusion from the Federal Labor Relations Act. All of the grower's motions were unsuccessful.

Meanwhile, depositions taken of the Salinas Strawberries leadership produced equivocal, contradictory and, therefore, embarrassing testimony about the reason for firing the workers. They had no answer for either the anonymous letters or the "fired for union activities" records unveiled to the hostile executives who had derided them before contentious depositions. Salinas Strawberries finally agreed to CRLA's demand to rehire the workers, pay them all missed wages and provide free rent and utilities for the period from the discharge to reinstatement. Further, Salinas Strawberries agreed it would never fire any of them ever again without showing "good cause." Word of the outcome spread like wild fire throughout the farmworker community in the Salinas Valley. Nothing like it had ever happened before.

César Chávez called to congratulate Marty and the Salinas staff for a precedent-setting win that protected workers' rights to organize. It was an ironic result, given that there had actually been no effort to organize by the workers who'd been fired.

The Salinas Strawberries case was just the beginning.

# Chapter 8
# MARTIN PRODUCE

Anthony Cervantes and Manual Ortiz were highly skilled machine tractor operators who, along with a crew of seven others, worked year-round for Martin Produce, Inc., a Salinas carrot farmer. Cervantes had been with Martin Produce for nine years and Ortiz had been there for seven. Ortiz, Cervantes and the others in the crew were by all accounts fine and valued workers. Both wanted higher pay and were concerned about the grower's disregard for health and safety laws, which required working conditions to be humane, that there be toilets in every field and sanitary drinking water. The laws also required pesticide spraying to be tightly controlled. California agribusinesses, important donors to Governor Ronald Reagan's campaign, claimed that compliance with these laws put them at a disadvantage in competing with producers from states without similar regulations. Many of these agribusinesses disregarded the laws with impunity.

Ortiz and Cervantes joined the United Farm Worker Union on July 26, 1967, and quietly started encouraging other workers in their crew to do the same. Another seven also joined up with the UFW by the end of July 1967. By joining, the workers knew they risked losing their jobs and being blackballed on other farms in the Salinas Valley. They ranged in age: Ortiz was the senior employee at 54 and Ignacio Burgos, the junior, at 22; José Pérez, 42, had ten years of seniority at Martin Produce and Jesús Robles had been there for eight years. The others were Antonio Casteñada, Domingo Longoria, Fred Wetherton and John Watson, the latter two African Americans.

On July 31, Martin Produce president John Martin, Jr., learned from a source about Cervantes' organizing efforts for the UFW. He promptly fired Cervantes. Martin immediately contacted Jim Houseberg at Grower-Shipper to report the union activity at his carrot farm, and Houseberg drove straight over. He had Ortiz pulled out of the carrot fields and hauled into Martin's office where Houseberg and Martin confronted him. Houseberg, introduced to Ortiz as the "head of the growers," demanded to know if Ortiz, as the senior crewmember, had also joined "that union."

Fearful for his job and the jobs of his friends, Ortiz denied that he or anyone else in his crew had joined any union. In his declaration filed later, Ortiz stated, "Houseberg took complete charge of the meeting, interrogated me at length, and said, 'All who join the union will be fired. The Chávez union has no power in Salinas. Go back and tell the boys that if they join the union, they will be fired and replaced by a new crew in two days.'"

Meanwhile, Cervantes went to the CRLA office and spoke to Bob Gnaizda. Bob gave Cervantes the bad news: "Since you were the only crew member fired, I don't think we can help you. They'll just make up some excuse and deny what they did. Come back if you learn Martin acts against any other workers." Bob was unaware at the time of the warnings Houseberg and Martin were communicating to Ortiz back at the carrot farm.

Undaunted by the threats made against them and the discharge of Cervantes, Martin Produce workers continued to organize quietly and urged other workers to join the United Farm Workers. On August 8, Martin received a telegram from the UFW seeking recognition for the carrot workers at his farm. Martin conferred again with Houseberg and with Ben López, Director of the Farm Labor Association; again he confronted his machine crew and demanded to know if they were union members. This time, Ortiz spoke up and said that they all were members and that it was their right to be in a union. Notwithstanding the seniority of the crew and the fact that they were the only machine crew working for the carrot farm at that time and were needed in the fields, the eight men were immediately fired and escorted off the farm.

Ortiz called Cervantes, who said they should all go together at once to CRLA. On August 10, the entire group traveled to the CRLA Salinas office to tell Marty and Bob what had happened. Bob contacted Martin at the carrot company and demanded the workers be immediately reinstated. "Or", he said, "be sued." Martin, while admitting nothing, told Bob he was sorry, but his hands were tied because he could not buck all the other growers. Marty went to work drafting a complaint, again relying on Section 923 of the labor code.

On August 25, 1967, CRLA brought suit against Martin Produce for the wrongful firing in violation of the California Labor Code. But Martin was not the only target of their lawsuit. In the same case, Marty and Bob, on behalf of the fired Martin carrot crew workers, sued the two Salinas grower associations and Houseberg personally for engaging in a "willful and malicious conspiracy, in knowing violation of law to deprive the workers of their right to organize and associate without reprisal."

The grower defendants hired Andy Church, a local attorney who represented many area farmers and was the son of Bruce Church, the principal owner of a large Salinas agricultural company, Bruce Church, Inc. (Indeed, Bruce Church, Inc. was a partner in the ownership of Salinas Strawberries.) Church asked Superior Court Judge Gordon Campbell to dismiss the case. On October 27, Judge Campbell issued his order refusing the request, finding that the complaint stated a cause of action and that it should proceed. Discovery commenced.

Martin Produce was represented by erstwhile CRLA antagonist and flame-thrower Bill Moreno. Moreno confided to CRLA attorneys that, after John Martin had suffered through his deposition and been forced to admit what he and Houseberg had done and that the fired workers were excellent workers who had done nothing wrong (other than joining the union). He said that his client wanted to move on. Moreno asked what it would take to get the experienced crew back to work at Martin Produce and the lawsuit against Martin concluded. No longer an avowed CRLA enemy, Moreno had come to Bob and Marty with hat in hand. In the negotiations that followed, the CRLA lawyers were unrelenting in undoing the harm caused to the carrot workers and setting an important example.

On December 7, 1967, Martin Produce hired back all nine workers, gave them back their full seniority, paid them $6750 in damages and affirmed that they could organize collectively if they wished. In addition, Martin promised them lifetime jobs, subject only to good-faith discharge (with arbitration if a dispute arose), and guaranteed them a continuing wage at least equal to the average of what they had been earning annually before their discharge: $4500.

Before the Martin settlement, the deposition of Ben López had zeroed in on the policies of the Farm Labor Association against the United Farm Worker Union. López had refused categorically to answer some 31 probing questions about the policies, and on December 22, Judge Campbell ordered López to respond fully to all of the questions. Meanwhile, Houseberg and the Farm Labor Association moved for summary judgment, claiming the case was moot because the workers had their jobs back as part of the settlement with Martin Produce. Superior Court Judge Brazil agreed with the association. CRLA appealed the dismissal of their case against the remaining defendants. A unanimous Court of Appeals panel in a precedent-setting opinion reversed the decision, affirmed that Labor Code Section 923 applied and sent the case against Houseberg and the Farm Labor Association back to the Superior Court for trial. This effectively curtailed the association's attempts to intimidate the workers. The matter was resolved confidentially soon afterward without need for resumption of the Ben López deposition.

# Chapter 9
# THE BRACERO CASE

Manuel Ortiz and the Martin Produce crew, within days of the carrot workers' suit, became involved in one of the most important and explosive lawsuits CRLA filed in its first ten years.

The Bracero Program was established in 1951 by Public Law 78 as an extension of the prior guest worker program instituted between the United States and Mexico in 1941. (The Spanish term *bracero* is translated as "one who works using his arms.") It was a United States government-sanctioned compact between US agricultural employers and the country of Mexico. In the ten years between its enactment and 1961, some 3,300,000 workers were brought into the country from Mexico to harvest crops in California, Texas, Florida and other agricultural states. While Public Law 78 terminated in 1964 during the Kennedy presidential administration, growers were still able to bring in workers under the H-2 program and were doing so as if Public Law 78 were still in effect. The captive H-2 *bracero* workers, while promised minimum wages and other benefits, had little ability to enforce their rights; reports of overworking and underpaying the workers and disregarding safety and housing laws were rampant. At that time, most of the major grower community depended on the guaranteed supply of a docile, foreign workforce. Curbing the use of *braceros* taking jobs from American citizens and green-card holders and depressing their wages was an early CRLA high priority.

Marty and Bob reviewed carefully the Department of Labor H-2 rules and regulations that set forth the federal approvals and certifications required for crews of *braceros* to be imported into the

United States. The rules specified a guaranteed minimum number of working weeks, minimum pay, fully compliant working conditions, free transportation and free housing for the imported workers. Critically, the rules required that growers *first* offer to American workers the same guaranteed wages and period of employment, benefits, free housing, transportation and working conditions. After investigation, the Secretary of Labor was required to certify that there were not enough available, able, willing and qualified US workers before foreign workers would be brought in to accomplish the harvest.

An additional requirement was that bringing in H-2 workers would not "depress the wages and working conditions of US workers." The required evidence had to be submitted to the Department of Labor by H-2 applicants in advance of the harvest; the applicants had to show their efforts and inability to attract domestic workers at the specified wages and benefits, including free housing and transportation and compliance with all rules.

Throughout California, various organizations representing growers, such as the Grower-Shipper Vegetable Organization in Salinas, handled the paperwork for individual growers, including Martin Produce. Marty and Bob began looking into the growers' compliance with the law. The CRLA community workers set about interviewing Ortiz and his crewmates, none of whom had ever heard of a farmer offering guaranteed wages. With the harvest about to begin, Marty and Bob concluded that this issue could be the first major inroad into an effective attack on the importation of *braceros*. They would sue Martin Produce and the United States Department of Labor in order to seek an order that their clients be hired to work at Martin Produce instead of the *braceros*. A few days later, the Secretary of Labor declared a labor shortage and authorized 8,000 *braceros* be brought into California. It was business as usual for the well-oiled machine run by the grower organizations and the Mexican government.

Marty and Bob filed their case, *Ortiz v. Wirtz,* on the morning of September 8, 1967, in San Jose Federal Court and asked for an expedited hearing for an injunction to require that their clients be hired, housed and paid for Martin Produce harvest work instead of the requested *bracero* laborers. Federal Judge Robert Peckham signed an Order to Show Cause, setting a hearing for ten days later. The case was Northern District of California No. 47803 RFP.

CRLA in the summer of 1967 was still a fledgling organization, and coordination between CRLA offices was not perfect. This was never more evident than with this case. The Salinas office lawyers were unaware that Sheldon Greene in the Modesto office was coordinating with CRLA attorney Gary Bellow in the McFarland office to also bring a suit against the Bracero Program for a group of farmworker clients in Kern County. Nor had Bellow and Greene heard about the Salinas office suit.

Unlike the Salinas case, the Modesto/McFarland case was unlimited in scope; it was a wholesale attack on the H-2 program brought on the eve of the harvest of California's multi-billion-dollar industry of lettuce, broccoli, tomatoes and other perishables having a short window to get from the fields to the packers, shippers, wholesalers, retailers and consumers. That suit asked to bring it all to a halt. Greene filed this second *bracero* case in the District Court in San Francisco and asked for a temporary restraining order to halt the use of any *braceros* in California in 1967. Greene also filed his suit on September 8, 1967, about four hours after Marty and Bob had filed their case in San Jose. Greene drew Judge Stanley Weigel and asked him to issue a temporary restraining order to halt all import and use of *braceros* until a hearing on the facts alleged in his case, *Alaniz v Wirtz,* had been held. That case became Northern District of California No. 47807 SAW.

Judge Weigel, a President Kennedy appointee, was a cantankerous and crusty Montana native, World War II Lieutenant and registered Republican. He was also a self-avowed social liberal. While in private practice in downtown San Francisco before his appointment to the bench, he had courageously taken on the unpopular case of some thirty-nine University of California professors who had refused to sign anti-Communist loyalty oaths in the McCarthy era.

Judge Weigel feared no one and nothing. He issued the requested restraining order, temporarily stopping the importation of *braceros.* At the same time, he proclaimed to Greene, in his own caustic style, that very substantial proof had better be forthcoming from CRLA at the hearing he set for a few days later if his temporary ban were to continue (and the lawyers who brought the case were to survive his wrath). As a result, some 8,000 foreign workers were placed on hold near the Mexican border.

The order was nothing less than a front-page bombshell proclaiming that the California harvest was stalled and in jeopardy of an unprecedented catastrophe. Within a few hours, the two federal judges learned that CRLA had filed *two different cases* in their courts, on the same day, both attacking the Bracero Program. To say the very least, they were not amused about what they saw to be a deliberate and manipulative tactic. They thus communicated to CRLA counsel in no uncertain terms that they were going to combine the two cases under the first filed *Ortiz* case number and name, and the hearing on the two consolidated orders to show cause would become the responsibility of the two Salinas lawyers.

When Bob and Marty checked in with Gary Bellow and his colleagues in McFarland, they learned that affidavits for the complainant domestic workers in the *Alaniz* case simply did not exist. And, there was no possibility of assembling them on a statewide basis in just a few days.

David Urdan, the Assistant US Attorney in San Francisco, who had been assigned to handle the *Ortiz* case for the United States Department of Labor, had been contacted as a courtesy by Marty on the day before he filed the case. That first call had been to describe the *Ortiz* case and see if the Labor Department would cooperate with the schedule proposed. They had quickly reached an agreement on that. Then, to his surprise, US Attorney Urdan called Marty back the next day, after he had been served with the restraining order in *Alaniz*.

"What in the hell is going on?" he asked Glick. "Why did we ever bother to cooperate with you, when you concealed that you were filing two cases? All bets are off."

"I had no idea whatsoever that another case would be filed," explained Marty, thoroughly embarrassed. "It was never our completely crazy idea to file two separate cases. Of course I would never have called you if we deliberately filed the two. I'm as surprised as you are, but I'm still ready to work with you now to see if we can resolve this whole thing right away."

The US attorney listened and calmed down somewhat, but then warned, "You can bet there will be no meeting unless you agree first that bringing in foreign workers can go forward in 1967 without obstruction to the harvest."

Taken aback, Marty responded, "A pre-condition is unacceptable. But we can drop the ban on foreign labor coming into California for this harvest, as long as your side commits to a discussion of real reforms and compliance with the rules and regulations after this season. American workers cannot be sidelined as a tactic for growers with no interest in collective bargaining and the better wages that come with it."

"Let me check with the Labor Department," the attorney answered, "and I'll call you back."

After three tense days of silence, US Attorney Urdan called back and said, "Okay, we'll meet, if it's up here in our offices. . . . So long as you understand that the first thing on our agenda is getting the *braceros* brought in and the crops picked and out to market this season."

They agreed to meet on those terms.

Marathon meetings at the US attorney's office ensued. On one side were five attorneys from the Departments of Labor and Justice out of Washington, DC, and the local office of US attorney; on the other side were Marty Glick and Bob Gnaizda. The clock continued to count down to the day of reckoning in a San Jose courtroom as the contours of an agreement began to take shape. The San Francisco federal team had to run ideas and language past the head office in Washington, DC, and thus progress was agonizingly slow.

Marty and Bob knew full well that there was no chance of the 1967 harvest use of *bracero* labor being aborted because the McFarland office case asking for that had been filed so late in the season that growers would have no way of getting the crops picked in time to avoid massive losses. CRLA, lacking the dynamite level of proof they would need to convince a federal judge to order such drastic action, had to play high-stakes poker with a losing hand, hoping that its bluff would not be called. The pair of CRLA lawyers, feigning reluctance indicated in the discussions that they would stand aside as to the 1967 harvest, if all parties would agree on full-bore compliance for 1968 and the years thereafter.

The Department of Labor representatives were seeking credit for a solution to the immediate harvest crisis. After initial remonstrations that CRLA had no right to demand anything whatsoever of Labor, the department concluded that it was not such a problem to commit themselves in some detail to how in 1968 and subsequent seasons it would actually enforce the regulations. The officials admitted that the Department of Labor had not really dotted the i's and crossed all the t's in making their certification that year, as it clearly had not. Early in the negotiation, Labor's commitments were emerging; including proof of offering to domestic workers guaranteed wages and free housing. In addition to Labor's willingness to put in writing how the department would enforce the regulations in succeeding years, it eventually agreed to Marty and Bob's demands that henceforth the Department of Labor would conduct public hearings on broad-based requests for foreign labor. The DOL would appoint a formal Regulation H-2 Advisory Committee with César Chávez and Bert Corona (both CRLA board members) as official members of the committee. The responsibilities of the committee would include review, before the next harvest, of the applicable rules and regulations and, indeed, the program itself. As the negotiations continued, Marty and Bob provided progress reports by phone to Bellow and a group of farmworkers assembled in the CRLA McFarland office. At about one in the morning on Monday, September 18, Bob and Marty signed a "Twelve Point Agreement" for CRLA's clients with the US Department of Labor eight hours before the scheduled hearing in San Jose. Lead US Attorney Urdan had done a good job of achieving his objective, resumption of the harvest. The fact that there was an agreed end to the case would allow the harvest to go forward. At the same time, the US Attorney and Labor Department team members were exhausted, having worked all day and night on Sunday. They asked Marty if he would provide a copy of the agreement to the court in the morning and ask Judge Peckham to "please excuse their non-appearance all the way down in San Jose" in light of the late night and weekend conclusion of the talks. "We are not really needed in the San Jose courthouse," they assured Marty.

Marty and Bob, not at all averse to being the sole messengers, agreed to convey their sentiments and take the signed agreement to the court and file it. Marty and Bob drove down to San Jose after the meeting concluded. Bob insisted that they stop in an all-night store on the way.

"We need to buy a ribbon and embossed seal to attach to the signed document to make it more special," Bob said.

Marty nodded.

Bob went on, "And when you introduce the settlement to the court and the press, you need to be sure to describe it as the 'Magna Carta' for farmworkers," Marty responded, "There is no way I am ever referring to this as any 'Magna Carta' . . . and I am not calling it a new amendment to the Bill of Rights either. Get serious. You know we'll have to fight this battle all over again next year. But the seal and ribbon is a cool idea."

They found a store that had what looked like a party favor: a gold seal with two red ribbons coming down around it. They bought it and, with some tape, attached the seal and ribbons to a copy of the signed stipulation and settlement. It was quite a sight when it was held up in court.

By 8 a.m. the next morning, the downtown San Jose courthouse and courtroom was mobbed by press representatives and attorneys for the growers. They were buzzing about like bees emerging from a disturbed hive, ready with motions to intervene in the litigation, clamoring to get the attention of the court clerk so they could lodge their motions. There were two wooden counsel tables with three chairs at each in front of the courtroom; Bob and Marty took their seats at the one marked "Plaintiff's Counsel." The other table for the defendant, the United States Department of Labor, was vacant. The elongated fourteen-chair jury box to the left was filled with members of the press. Television crews had set up in the hallway, awaiting the anticipated courtroom fireworks.

At 9 a.m., the courtroom deputy asked all to rise as the judge entered the courtroom and took the bench. Judge Peckham asked impatiently, "Where is the United States attorney?"

Marty rose and announced, holding up the ribbon-decorated copy with the $2.50 gold seal, "Your honor, we are pleased to announce we have a signed agreement settling this case, reached very early this morning in San Francisco."

There was a collective gasp in the courtroom at that point.

Marty Glick continued by informing the court of the request by the assistant US attorney to convey the reasons for his absence.

Judge Peckham was livid at the non-appearance and announced, "This is unacceptable. This is not the first time this court has been disrespected by the Office of the United States Attorney, but I am going to see to it this is the last time it will occur without sanctions. San Jose is a fully legitimate part of the Northern District jurisdiction, and lawyers for the United States need to learn their geography."

Then, Judge Peckham told his clerk to inform the US attorney of his displeasure.

With that issue behind him, Judge Peckham turned again towards counsel table and asked, "Mr. Glick, can you please hand the clerk the stipulation and settlement papers so I can review them?"

Marty handed the signed document (a plain vanilla no-seal copy) to the clerk, who in turn took it to the bench. Judge Peckham proceeded to read the document, carefully and quietly, as he remained on the bench in the hushed courtroom. After finishing his review, the Judge announced, "This settlement seems thorough and fair and is accepted by the court. I am very pleased you have achieved a resolution. Mr. Glick, as you can see, we have a very full courtroom today. As one of the counsel for the farmworker plaintiffs, and since the government did not bother to show up, I now direct you to read the agreement out loud to all present in the courtroom, please."

As Marty began to read the document aloud in the packed courtroom, he realized just how impressive in its detail and content it sounded, especially to anyone not familiar with existing regulations. He slowed and increased emphasis as he got to the provisions about the guaranteed wages and housing for domestic workers, the required public hearings and the new committee with César Chávez and Bert Corona. The growers' shock, dismay, frustration and fury at the settlement was unmistakable.

When the reading was completed, Judge Peckham ignored the entreaties of those who were still seeking intervention and objecting. He reiterated that he was satisfied and ready to approve dismissal of the case based on the stipulation. He signed with a flourish, gave it to his clerk to file and announced, "This case is completed," then left the bench.

In the hallway afterward, Bob held forth with the media and, more than once, Marty heard references to the ancient document signed by King John of England in the year 1215.

That day and in the days that followed, the growers complained bitterly to the Labor Department, Governor Reagan and the other California legislators they supported with campaign contributions from the farm counties in California. Republican Congressman Charles Gubser, representing the 10th Congressional District stretching from Livermore to Vacaville, pronounced that the settlement was "a surrender document . . . a new low in groveling submission to blackmail by an agency of the US Government . . . a tribute to a rump organization."

Democratic Congressman Bernie Sisk, representing Fresno and other Central Valley counties, thundered that the DOL had "rolled over and played dead."

California Senator George Murphy took to the Senate floor and demanded sanctions against CRLA and declared that the organization should have "no business in our farm affairs . . . .The citizens of California are horrified by the spectacle of CRLA lawyers, paid for by their tax dollars, going to court against the Secretary of Labor and his Justice Department."

A month earlier, CRLA Modesto attorney Sheldon Greene had filed a class-action lawsuit that successfully and permanently enjoined some $210 million in Reagan-administration Medi-Cal cuts that clearly violated federal laws. With the two landmark victories, CRLA had earned the unrelenting enmity of Governor Reagan, Senator Murphy and their confederates. Apparently, acting as effective attorneys for indigents in enforcing the law against elected officials was both unprecedented and somehow unacceptable.

Following the outcome of the settlement with the Department of Labor, CRLA carefully monitored for H-2 requests made to the Labor Department the following year. A field team of community workers in every CRLA office coordinated by attorney Ed Mattison and by community worker Father Zo Avila, collected declarations from farmworkers. On September 11, 1968, at a press conference held in St. Mary's Church in Stockton, CRLA attorney Greene presented the findings and proof that, once again, domestic workers had not been offered the required jobs, wages, benefits and working conditions. Marty had written to Secretary Wirtz a week earlier to ask when there would be compliance with the stipulation; he also met in San Francisco with Labor Department Regional Administrator Glenn Brockway and his lawyers on the day of the Stockton press conference to share the declarations with them. The Labor Department made excuses as to why the required advisory committee hearings had not yet been held but pointed out that there were no requests for foreign workers. Marty also wrote to Vice-President Humphrey on September 10, asking him to intervene at the DOL if it received any such requests. Humphrey wrote back that, "There are no formal requests by the growers now pending before the Department of Labor."

For the first time since 1942, California agriculture did not import *braceros*. Thus did the H-2 version of the Bracero Program end.

# Chapter 10
## THE LITERACY CASE

From the beginning, CRLA was a legal juggernaut with a record of accomplishments that won it the inaugural award from the Office of Economic Opportunity as the "Most Outstanding Legal Services Program" in the nation. While by no means did CRLA lawyers prevail in all of their significant cases, they were often successful. CRLA achieved many of its victories in the California Supreme Court and the other appellate courts in California.

One of the early cases involved the right of literate but non-English-speaking citizens to vote in California. *Castro v. California* was brought by a young CRLA attorney, Don Kates, who before joining CRLA had studied election and voting laws as well as early California history. In 1967, CRLA's Healdsburg office represented two quite literate Spanish-speaking native-born clients who had been denied the right to vote because of the English-language literacy requirement in the California Constitution at the time. Kates, then headquartered in the central CRLA office in Los Angeles, teamed up with prominent constitutional lawyers in Los Angeles; they represented Genoveva Castro in a class-action attack on the literacy requirement.

The petition Kates' team filed began by tracing the racist, anti-Catholic origin of the English-literacy requirement. In 1850, California entered the Union with two official languages, Spanish and English, and there was no literacy requirement of any kind as a precondition to voting. English-language literacy became a requirement in 1894, passed by the California Assembly out of clearly articulated prejudice against Catholics immigrating in large numbers from Southern and Eastern Europe, as well as the Chinese and other foreigners. The anti-immigrant wave at the time was fueled by the American Protective Association and the Immigration Restriction League. The law, commonly known as the "Bledsoe Amendment," honored Assemblyman A. J. Bledsoe, a leader of a mob that had expelled all Chinese from Humboldt County in 1889. Bledsoe openly modeled his proposed amendment on requirements used to deny African Americans the right to vote in Mississippi and elsewhere in the South. He and his supporters said repeatedly that the groups to be excluded were "unlettered and un-American aliens," "ignorant and vicious foreigners," "debased and ignorant Europeans" and "aliens as vile as and more numerous than even the heathen Chinese, the encroaching swarms from portions of Europe." Enacted in 1894 as Article II, Section 1 of the Constitution, the new provision sponsored by Bledsoe provided that, "No person who shall not be able to read the constitution in the English language and read and write his or her own name shall ever [vote]."

In an opinion authored by Justice Sullivan for a unanimous California Supreme Court, the English-language literacy requirement was struck down as a denial of equal protection under the 14th Amendment to the United States Constitution. The final paragraph of that historic decision read as follows:

> We cannot refrain from observing that if a contrary conclusion were compelled, it would indeed be ironic that petitioners [Hispanic citizens], who are the heirs of a great and gracious culture identified with the birth of this culture and contributing in no small measure to its growth, should be disenfranchised in their ancestral land despite their capacity to cast an informed vote.

# Chapter 11
## SALINAS ACTIVITY BEFORE THE *DIANA* CASE

After their early successes in 1967, CRLA had no shortage of clients and client organizations asking for help, and the major case activity in that office rolled on. In 1967, Bob became Director of Litigation for CRLA, and Marty took over as Directing Attorney of the Salinas office. In 1968, Marty and Bob filed a case entitled *250 Farmworkers v. Schultz and the California Employment Department,* which demanded the institution of a new Fair Employment Plan or the closure of the 42 state-run Farm Labor Service offices scattered around rural California. The complaint alleged that the federally funded Farm Labor Service, established by the California Employment Development Department (EDD), was a captive of the growers, that it never consulted with employee groups and that, knowingly, in clear violation of regulations for the protection of farm laborers, it referred workers to growers who were in persistent violation of wage, health and safety laws. Growers served by the Farm Labor Service included those who had a record of (1) spraying fields with pesticides while farmworkers were still in them; (2) failing to provide toilets in the field, let alone separate ones for females; (3) not providing adequate drinking water for workers often laboring in high heat; and (4) ignoring minimum wage requirements. William Tolbert, then secretary of the California Farm Labor Service (and formerly an executive of the Ventura County Citrus Growers Association), testified that it was not the responsibility of any of his 316-state agency employees of the Farm Labor Service to assure that minimum wages were paid or health and safety laws were observed in the private sector.

Discovery in that case revealed that Farm Labor Service senior employees had met with prominent growers and grower organizations often, but had virtually never met with or consulted with workers or worker organizations. Federal District Judge Alfonso Zirpoli ordered the EDD to "submit a plan" in 90 days for revision of the Farm Labor Service operations covering seven broad principles. These principles included the public listing of all jobs, field conditions and pesticide applications. Also included were provisions for field spot checks and advisory committees that included farmworker representatives. The required changes were implemented and, within four years, the Farm Labor Service wing of EDD was closed down permanently.

In another case, Marty represented two workers, Gregoria Zermeño, 65, and Mary García, 53, who were denied unemployment insurance because, allegedly, they were unavailable for work, despite the fact that they had worked in California for decades, were actively seeking new work and were otherwise fully qualified to receive the benefits they had earned on their jobs. Zermeño had lived in Monterey County since 1922 and García had been in the county since 1930. Their benefits had been denied solely because they were undocumented workers.

The Unemployment Insurance Appeals Board reversed the denial in July 1968 and granted both of them benefits, holding that the denial was unconstitutional. The board noted it was for the Attorney General and the immigration service to deal with status issues and not for the Employment Development Department to make judgments about who was or was not "legal."

In the fall of 1968, the Atascadero School District, in order to reduce costs, curtailed its school bus system. Atascadero was a country village about 100 miles south of Salinas and 100 miles north of Santa Barbara. The school district decided it would no longer provide buses to school from labor camps, where farmworker families resided. Bob and Marty filed suit in the San Luis Obispo court to overrule the Atascadero school board decision. They successfully argued that, while it was the School District's right to reduce the cost of educating children, the United States

Constitution does not allow this to be done by eliminating the ability of poor children to get to the schoolhouse.

Not long after the Atascadero case, CRLA undertook another education case, this time in the small town of Gonzales, just nine miles north of Soledad. One Monday evening while two recent Hastings Law School graduates CRLA had just hired—Ralph Abascal and Mo Jourdane—were seeing clients in Soledad, Guillermo and Paula Sánchez came into the office. Ralph knew who they were because their son Francisco was a ranked California high school track athlete with one of the fastest recorded times in the mile. Ralph had met the family before and even attended a county track meet.

"*Señor Abogado*," said Mr. Sánchez, speaking in Spanish, "I know you know our son and that he is a strong runner, but he is also on his way to college, thanks to his teacher, *Señora* Paula Alvarez. She is now in trouble because she helps Mexican students like our Francisco. Mr. Fear, our principal, wants to fire *Señora* Alvarez for encouraging Mexican boys and girls to go to college. She is the first and only Mexican teacher in the history of Gonzales High School, and we would like to see her be protected."

Attorney Abascal was the grandson of a stonemason from Santander, Spain. His father, Manuel, had gone from Spain to Cuba, worked on the railroad in northwest Mexico, then crossed the border at Tijuana and settled in San Diego, where Ralph was born. Ralph, after a stint as a blackjack dealer in Reno, ultimately earned a master's degree in business at the University of California in Berkeley. He was very articulate and comfortable in both Spanish and English. Jourdane, still learning Spanish, was doing his best to keep up with the rapid back and forth. Ralph told the Sánchez family that he and Mo would look into the issue right away.

The next day, Ralph and Mo drove to Gonzales to meet with Ms. Alvarez. When they arrived, they were surprised to find not only Francisco Sánchez but also another twenty-three Mexican-American students who had come there to rally around their teacher. The whole group entered Classroom 12, where Paula Alvarez was waiting. As Mo started to introduce himself and Ralph, Ms. Alvarez interrupted to say she already knew who they were. She smiled and said that Francisco had already told her that Mo was a new guy, a long-haired, surfer lawyer, and she had seen "Rafael" around Gonzales before and heard he was a friend of the community. She also said she knew about and trusted CRLA. The two lawyers advised the students to wait outside to protect the attorney-client relationship and then asked Ms. Alvarez to describe the problem.

"They say I am guilty of 'false expectations,'" she said. "It's crazy."

"What do they mean by 'false expectations?'" asked Mo.

"Ten years ago," she said, "I was a student here and none of us Mexicans were ever expected to go to college. I got the ambition to become a teacher myself and change all that, and I was hired last fall. This spring, the students started a MECHA Chapter. It's the Mexican American Chicano Association. They chose me to be their advisor. I encouraged and tutored the MECHA members to continue their education after graduation, to go to college. Thirty-one took the SAT, the test for college that I helped them to prepare for.

"It was an amazing success as every student got a high enough score to go on to higher education, many to Hartnell, the local college in Salinas, some to San Jose State and one even got a scholarship to UC Berkeley. I thought the school administration would be thrilled and maybe give me an award."

"And?" Ralph asked.

"*Ni siquiera*," she replied. "It was the opposite. In April, Principal Fear marched into my classroom after the students had left for the day. I could see he was angry. Looking down at me, he said, 'You're making a mistake pumping up the self-image of your Mexican-American students. Yes, some will go to college, but you know they will flunk out by Christmas. Don't you know they should just want to work in the fields so they can get new cars? But you're pressuring them to go to college. False expectations is what you have created.'"

"Unbelievable," said Mo. "What did you say?"

"'*Basta* [enough],' is what I said. I'd heard enough. I told him to get out of my classroom. Since then, everything I do they say I do wrong. I was two minutes late to the faculty meeting—I got a warning. I went to the hospital without leaving a lesson plan when my little girl got hit by a car—I got another warning. Yesterday, I got notice they won't need me next year."

CRLA filed suit. Several weeks later, a federal judge ordered the Gonzales High School District to reinstate Ms. Alvarez until a hearing on the merits could proceed. Presumably the Monterey County Counsel Office told the Gonzales school officials that it was going to be a steep uphill battle to sustain a discharge on the basis of "false expectations," so they relented and agreed to make the reinstatement of Ms. Alvarez permanent.

# Chapter 12
## CALL ME PANCHO

Another early CRLA initiative involved the cavalier treatment of farmworkers by the Immigration and Naturalization Service (INS). Following up on a series of complaints, Marty visited the United States Consulate in Tijuana and reported to the INS mistreatment of farmworker applicants there, where some had to camp outside the office for days without even being acknowledged, despite the fact that they had appointments. The INS agreed to investigate and make changes.

But by far, the most frequent complaints received by the CRLA about INS agents concerned the singling out and detention of Mexican Americans without cause, costing them work and wages and fostering a climate of fear among citizens and green card holders. Bob contacted the INS District Office in San Francisco and asked if the agency head would come to a meeting with workers in Salinas to discuss these and other issues.

INS District Director Cecil Fullilove agreed to travel to Salinas to hear from them. Bob arranged for a Salinas school auditorium and had the community workers organize a group of 30 to 40 to attend and ask questions. Bob also invited Eric Brazil of the Salinas *Californian* newspaper to be at the meeting.

When Fullilove arrived and was introduced to the *Californian* reporter, he became upset that a member of the press was present. He angrily complained, "This is not okay. You all are attempting to ambush me, and I am not going to stand for it. There will be no meeting, and I'm leaving."

In an effort to get a dialogue going and find some common ground, Bob said, "Sorry, that was not our intent. Please hang on and listen to at least one member of the community tell about his experiences."

Without waiting for an answer, Marty called on Lyle Pineda, who earnestly explained, "Honorable sir, thank you for coming. My complaint is that immigration officers without reason stop me and demand to see my papers. They call me 'Pancho,' even though I tell them my name is Lyle and not Pancho. . . . Many of the federal immigration agents call every Mexican they stop 'Pancho,' and it is disrespectful."

Fullilove rose, steaming and purple-faced, with his briefcase in hand. He said loudly and emphatically, "I see no problem whatsoever with that. I happen to know that Mexican Americans like to be called Pancho!" With that, he buttoned his coat and departed from the meeting and Salinas.

Bob Gnaizda, never at a loss for an off-the-charts idea, asked Lyle and some others in attendance to go out into the streets and conduct a survey of every Mexican American they could find and ask them their names and if they liked to be called Pancho, instead of being called by their real names. The secretarial staff quickly turned out an official-looking survey form on the letterhead of a 15-minute-old, newly minted (and memberless) organization named "Chicanos for Fair Treatment." Two hours later, Lyle and his team had stopped and interviewed about fifty Chicanos walking on Main Street. Of that group, forty-nine said they did not like or expect to be called Pancho instead of their real name. The fiftieth, a truck driver named Francisco, said he liked it just fine; not surprising, since Pancho is the nickname for Francisco.

Eric Brazil wrote up the story, and the Salinas *Californian* prominently carried the survey on the front page. It also mentioned that Fullilove had walked out of the meeting. Bob sent the story on to Labor Secretary Wirtz, Senator Cranston and various members of the California delegation in Congress. Within a week, high-level Labor officials flew from DC to Salinas to apologize. They patiently listened to the assembled group and reviewed the list of grievances. Among the agreed changes, the Border Patrol was directed not to address farmworkers indiscriminately as Pancho or to stop them without cause based only on their skin color or apparent nationality.

PART THREE
# 1969–1970
# THE *DIANA* CASE: ROUND ONE

# Chapter 13
## IQ TEST HISTORY

Interest in intelligence, and the animated debate about the degree to which it is a product of heredity versus environment, dates back to the nineteenth century. A British psychometrician, Francis Galton, set about in 1883 to prove that intelligence was entirely inherited and thus fixed, like eye color, by attempting to correlate intelligence to head size, reflex, grip and other observable physical traits. He created a standardized test and made several attempts to prove his hypothesized connection without success.

By the beginning of the twentieth century, educators in Europe began conducting tests to identify "mentally retarded" public school children. Accordingly, in 1905, Alfred Binet, a French psychiatrist, and his colleagues published and implemented the first test of the intelligence quotient test (IQ), known as the Binet-Simon test. Modern IQ tests have both a "verbal" section to test aptitude and the ability to comprehend and reason with words and a "non-verbal" or "performance" section, which tests ability to work with numbers, shapes and diagrams. The Binet test was entirely verbal with its results expressed as a measurement related to the age of the child. The Binet thesis, a fair one at least in this respect, was that the older the child, the more developed his or her brain and other physical attributes and exposure to life, learning and language would be; thus, a higher raw score was to be expected as the test taker became older. Test results were compared to standardized results from other subjects of the same age;

a score of 100 was defined as average. The test sample was of Caucasian children only.

While definitions of retardation have varied over the decades, the generally accepted view is that "retardation" is at least two standard deviations below the norm; therefore, a score on an IQ test of 70 or below, depending on the particular test, is an indication of possible retardation. The lower the score, the greater the "retardation."

Binet understood well and expressed openly the limitations of his test results; by themselves, they were not appropriate for establishing an individual's level of intelligence nor indicating that IQ was immutable. He stated,

> Some recent philosophers appear to have given their moral support to the deplorable verdict that the intelligence of an individual is a fixed quantity . . . we must protest. . . . A child's mind is like a field for which an expert farmer has advised a change in the method of cultivating, with the result that in the place of desert land, we now have a harvest.

Binet argued, "It is necessary to react against and protest the brutal pessimism of those who regard the test as measuring some fixed and unchanging quantity."

In 1916, Lewis Termin at Stanford University, using a translation of Binet's work, developed the Stanford-Binet Intelligence Test, still entirely verbal and based on a test sample entirely composed of Anglo-American children. Termin's views, however, were the diametric opposite of Binet's; Termin was a firm disciple of "eugenics," the belief that intelligence is entirely inherited and that the non-white races of the world possessed inferior intelligence and that their population should be curbed or involuntarily eliminated. Termin advocated that his test could accurately identify the "feeble-minded" so that authorities could discourage them from breeding. Termin asserted that racial and ethnic groups had higher percentages of defective children. In 1916, he proclaimed that borderline feeble-mindedness "is very, very common among Spanish-Indian and Mexican families in the Southwest and also among Negroes." He considered their "dullness" to be an inherited racial characteristic.

On the subject of schooling non-white children, Termin wrote, "These boys are uneducable beyond the merest rudiments of training. No amount of school instruction will ever make them intelligent voters or capable citizens in the true sense of the word. Judged psychologically, they cannot be considered normal." Termin went on to say that the low scorers on his test should be segregated in special classes. The revised Binet test, the Stanford-Binet, and many of Termin's conclusions—including the need to segregate—were very widely accepted in schools in the United States. In 1921, the then Superintendent of Public Instruction in California stated, "Undoubtedly, [the] high percentage of children enrolled in in the public schools who are definitely [as shown by Termin's test] feeble-minded was due, in part, to the predominance of a foreign-born population. . . . It is an extravagance to keep feeble-minded children in classes with other children."

Another prominent eugenicist in the early twentieth century was Henry Goddard, a professor at Princeton University. He conducted IQ tests on arriving immigrants at Ellis Island and found a correlation between ethnicity and lack of intelligence in a very high percentage of them: 83% of Jews, 87% of Russians, 80% of Hungarians and 79% of Italians were proved by his IQ tests to be "feeble-minded."

Further IQ research by believers in the notion that IQ is fixed at birth targeted the Spanish-speaking. One 1926 IQ study concluded, "All mental testing of Spanish-Mexican descent has shown that the average intelligence of this group is even lower than the average intelligence of the Portuguese and Negro children." That study also included Canadians: "From Canada . . . the increase of French-Canadians is alarming. . . . The average intelligence of the French-Canadian group in our data approaches the level of average Negro intelligence."

In the 1920s, several states enacted mandatory sterilization laws with subjects to be identified or confirmed by IQ tests. Notwithstanding criticism by opponents at the time of both the notion of fixed intelligence and of the biases and inadequacies of the Stanford-Binet test, some sixty to seventy thousand American women were forcibly sterilized pursuant to these state laws and the tests. In *Buck v. Beck*, the Supreme Court by a vote of 8-1 sustained Virginia's laws and permitted the sterilization of Carrie Buck.

The early test items on the Stanford-Binet were vocabulary, math, general knowledge and reasoning. Later, IQ non-verbal testing was developed for the United States Army so it could better test recruits with limited English-language skills and education.

In 1939, David Wechsler published his first IQ test (the "WISC") and instead of it concluding with just a single number result and being entirely verbal, his test, as revised over the years, had ten sub-categories: five verbal and five non-verbal. Wechsler, like Binet before him, was very clear about limitations in his testing:

> We have eliminated the colored vs. white factor by admitting from the outset that our norms cannot be used for the colored population of the United States. Our standardization is based upon white subjects only. We omitted the colored population from our first standardization because we feel that the items derived by mixing the population could not be interpreted without special provisos and reservations.

Weschler also did not include the Spanish-surnamed in his samples. By the 1960's, the WISC IQ test was the most common and popular test used in US schools and, notwithstanding the clear warning from its author, it was used indiscriminately for the testing of *all* children.

# Chapter 14
## THE FOUNDATION IS LAID FOR
## THE *DIANA* CASE

With so many young, inexperienced lawyers on the statewide CRLA staff, Marty had become one of the most experienced in major litigation. In late 1968, he was named CRLA Director of Litigation for the state and, in January 1969, moved to the CRLA central office in San Francisco, in the shadow of San Francisco City Hall and three blocks from the federal courts. Bob Gnaizda became a program deputy director and also joined the central office in San Francisco. Marty, as head of the CRLA Education Task Force, turned first to research and analysis of major California education issues.

The status quo for low-income minority and Spanish-speaking children in the California school system in 1967 was grim, especially for the children of farmworker families. Many children did not enter school speaking or understanding much of the English language, as Spanish was their native tongue. Few schools had teachers or other staff fluent in Spanish or familiar with either the culture or the needs of migrant or labor camp children. Farmworker parents lacked both time and the understanding of how to intervene at school on behalf of their children, so their children too often languished. Since children with limited language skills progressed slowly in regular classrooms, schools endeavored to track them off into separate classes, where expectations were low and quality instruction was lacking.

In 1972, the dropout rate before high school graduation in California among non-Latino whites was 12%, for blacks 22% and for Hispanics it was 34%! Students from low-income families were six times more likely to fail to graduate from high school than their high-income family counterparts. The set of statistics by race and ethnic background of children assigned to EMR classes jumped off the pages of the many reports provided by the California Department of Education. In the 1966-67 school year, Spanish surname students were about 13% of the total public school population but constituted double that rate, some 26%, of the EMR class population, what in essence was an overrepresentation by about 13,000 students.

CRLA's initial priority was to learn how students were placed in these classes and what could be done about the disparity. The task force quickly learned that assignment to EMR classes in California resulted almost entirely from teacher referral for IQ testing. Thus, it became essential to look into IQ testing and administration. Marty researched the checkered history of the development, uses and abuses of those tests.

In the 1960s and early 1970s, schools in California administered a so-called "Group IQ Test" to all third graders. Although they mirrored group achievement tests that measured how much a student had actually learned, the IQ label was pernicious because the scores went into individual student files, biased teacher perceptions of particular students' ability to learn and affected which students they might refer for further testing to see if they should be removed from a regular classroom setting.

The use of an IQ score as the primary or sole determinant of placement in classes for the Educable Mentally Retarded grew exponentially in the post-World War II period. Sample test questions included the following: "Why is it better to pay bills by check than with cash?" "What color are rubies?" "What is the meaning of C.O.D.?" "Where is Chile?" "What is a chattel?" "Who wrote Romeo and Juliet?" The test reflected Anglo-American middle-class culture and was normed on the knowledge it valued. It should not have been administered to students who had been raised in an entirely different culture or socio-economic context, much less to students who did not speak English or were in the process of learning the language.

In 1968, Dr. Uvaldo Palomares, then 32, had just published his historically important doctoral dissertation on misuse of culturally biased IQ tests and improper placement of large numbers of Mexican-American students into Imperial County EMR classes. Palomares, once on the road himself to special classes in elementary school, had instead been taken under the wing of a caring teacher who saw he was smart and skilled in the strategy of winning marbles from his classmates on the playground. Marty found Dr. Palomares' published dissertation and called him. At the time, Palomares was on the faculty at San Diego State University and was happy to share his findings in some detail. They discussed possible remedies. And then Palomares connected Marty to leaders of an emerging group that came to be named the California Association of Chicano Psychologists, and particularly to a man named Steve Moreno. Palomares later became one of the first three licensed Chicano psychiatrists in California.

The Association of Chicano Psychologists sent the Palomares study and other follow-up research on this question to the Department of Education in 1968 with demands for prompt change. In partial response, the California Department of Education commissioned a study of IQ testing on Mexican-American children. The study included retesting, with more culturally appropriate questions, a group of some 45 children. Published in 1969, it concluded that those children's IQ scores were not consistent with their true abilities. The California Department of Education ignored its own research.

The misuse of culturally biased testing and representation in classes for the retarded was by no means limited to Mexican-American children. The representation of African American children in these classes was even more disproportionate. The 1966-67 school year statistics showed that while blacks were 8% of the general California public school population, they represented 21% of all pupils in EMR classes. While African and Mexican-American students represented 21.5% of the population in general, they were collectively represented almost 48% of special education and EMR classes.

In August 1969, the California Assembly in Sacramento passed a resolution urging school districts to re-evaluate student assignments in light of the very high and disproportionate numbers of Mexican Americans in classes for the Educable Mentally Retarded. Notwithstanding the resolution by the legislature, protests from professional groups and the limitations and warnings voiced by the test authors themselves, nothing had changed by the end of the decade.

Indeed, despite the growing public awareness of these disparities, the California Department of Education actually moved aggressively in the opposite direction in 1969. Many of the behind-the-scenes decisions made by the department as it rushed to get particular IQ tests approved did not come to light until later in litigation. The history of classes for the retarded in California is instructive. State funding and establishment of special education EMR classes had begun in California in 1947. By 1951, classes for the Trainable Mentally Retarded (TMR) were also created for those who were severely developmentally impaired. Students were generally classified as TMR when they were at least three standard deviations below the norm or scored approximately 55 or lower on the IQ test. Enrollment in EMR classes had grown since these first special classes were established. It reached an all-time high in 1969 with about 58,000 students enrolled statewide. Nationally, there were about 725,000 children in EMR classes at the time.

The Department of Education passed a regulation in 1969 that established an approved list of IQ tests to use when evaluating whether a child should be placed in an EMR class. The state approved these IQ tests in only two months, July and August 1969, without outside sources consulted, other than California school psychologists, who were asked to identify what they were already using. Letters of protest about the procedure were received and ignored, and the WISC and Stanford-Binet tests were chosen, as well as the rarely used Leiter test, which had been developed primarily for the hearing-impaired and those with speech deficiencies. No hearings were ever held. No investigation of cultural or language bias was undertaken. The Department of Education did not heed the clear warnings of Albert Binet and David Wechsler nor did it consult representatives of minorities or independent experts of color.

Apparently, the state rushed to certify these IQ tests with the clear knowledge within the California Department of Education of the weaknesses, stigma and bias associated with the tests. They knew the tests would be used to place more Hispanic and black children into classes for the Educable Mentally Retarded, where they were already overrepresented.

To prepare for the serious legal challenge to come, Marty obtained from Palomares and Moreno copies of the Stanford-Binet and WISC to analyze what types of questions the tests asked and how they were formulated. CRLA would use this information, as well as expert studies of the tests, to prepare the details of the formal complaint they would file on behalf of the Soledad children.

Another task undertaken by CRLA was to study how local school districts were funded to understand the California Department of Education's and the School District's incentives and disincentives for assigning children to EMR classes. School funding included California and federal supplemental support (so-called categorical funds) for a variety of special programs and for certain targeted sub-groups of children. One such category was extra monies for the average daily attendance of children in EMR classes. Removal of children from such classes would cost the districts money and require resources to be invested by local and state authorities to help them to catch up. This was a significant issue considered by the task force.

By the Summer of 1969, CRLA was ready to go, and word was sent to the field offices to be on alert for Latino parents complaining about misplacement of their son or daughter in an EMR class. Now, CRLA just needed parents frustrated with the treatment of their children to understand that they could bring the issue to CRLA.

# Chapter 15
## MO JOINED CRLA

Positive or negative, much of what happens in life is serendipity. Conducting a search for new lawyers and interviewing them is time-consuming, and therefore the various CRLA leaders shared the responsibility. In the fall of 1967, it was Marty's turn to recruit summer interns for CRLA at Hastings College of Law in San Francisco. While interviewing second-year students who had signed up, he found the proverbial diamond in the rough. In walked Maurice "Mo" Jourdane. He was super bright and energetic. As Marty described CRLA to Mo, it was as if a light had turned on— Jourdane's smile illuminated the room. A few days later, Marty offered Mo the position, and he joined the CRLA summer program in McFarland a few weeks later.

Maurice Jourdane, whose grandparents had farmed grapefruit and avocados in rural San Diego County, grew up in Huntington Park, California. Huntington Park lies between Watts and East Los Angeles, six miles southeast of the Los Angeles City Hall. It changed in the 1910s and 1920s from grazing land to residential streets lined with wooden single-level two- and three-bedroom homes. When Mo was growing up, Huntington Park was a pocket of white lower-class families. Many were second-generation California Okies. Although part of the massive Los Angeles metropolis, it could have been any small town in America.

Mo, as a second-year law student, joined the CRLA office in McFarland near Delano, where César Chávez, Dolores Huerta and a handful of others were struggling to get the Farm Worker Union organized. He is and was unassuming, engaging, caring and empathetic. Underneath the personable exterior was a will of iron, an unrelenting energy and a razor-sharp mind quick to grasp difficult concepts and to find practical solutions. César Chávez and Dolores Huerta were consequently almost instantly attracted to the young law student and a lifetime friendship developed between them. After learning during his summer work that the National Labor Relations Act purposely excluded farmworkers, Jourdane returned to law school and published an article in the Hastings Law Review, "The Constitutionality of Exclusion of Farm Workers from the National Labor Relations Act." The law review article attacked the constitutionality of exclusions from the labor law that protected all workers except farmworkers and domestic workers, predominately workers of color. He sent a copy to César and Dolores.

Mo spent his final year of law school taking required classes in corporate and tax law in the morning and working at the local office of San Francisco Neighborhood Legal Assistance in the afternoon. Most of his clients were African American, but their everyday problems did not differ dramatically from those of the brown farmworkers he had met in California's fields. Mo was in San Francisco, but his mind and spirit were still in the San Joaquin Valley every time he thought of the issues faced by the stooped farmworkers he had seen and met the previous summer. He had received an offer of permanent employment back in McFarland from CRLA but had not accepted it. That spring, César Chavez himself called Mo to express his appreciation of Mo's easy understanding of farmworker needs and issues as reflected in the law review article. He urged Mo to accept a full-time job with California Rural Legal Assistance.

"I thought we could count on you to represent farmworkers," Chávez said.

"I enjoyed working with the workers, Mr. Chávez," Mo said. "A year ago, I gave up surfing for one summer. Now, you're asking me to give up waves indefinitely. All my life I have promised myself I would always live near the beach. With my own law office, I could live in Laguna and surf whenever I want. I just don't know if I can handle living in some place like Modesto or Delano."

Hearing César's voice, Mo recalled the laughing, dark-haired children playing along the bank of the Kern River and the farmworkers picketing a desolate grape field on the dusty road. "I really do want to be a lawyer for farmworkers, but I can't lose surfing. I have to live where I can surf. What Rural Legal Assistance offices are good and near the beach?"

"If you work in Santa Maria, you could live in Pismo Beach," Chávez answered.

Not much of a surf spot, Mo thought. It has the ocean and the sand dunes, but it's cold and windy.

As if reading Mo's thoughts, César said, "Gilroy is over the Santa Cruz Mountains from good surf, and Salinas is half an hour from Monterey Beach. Marty, who hired you as an intern, works there. Why don't you call Rural Legal Assistance and see if they'll let you work in Gilroy or Salinas?"

Mo did exactly that and accepted CRLA's job offer to work in the Salinas office. In the Fall of 1968, he joined CRLA full time.

When Mo arrived in Salinas, Marty and Bob were in the process of transitioning to the San Francisco central office, but the Salinas connection they all shared kept them in close communication and working together on many significant cases. One of those cases was the long-running and successful battle to outlaw the back crippling short-handled hoe or "El Cortito." The case is detailed in *The Struggle for the Health and Legal Protection of Farm Workers* published by Arte Público Press in 2004.

"Mo, we need someone to take over our Monday office hours in Soledad since I will be leaving here shortly. Call Hector de la Rosa down there. You'll love working with him and the clients there."

"Okay, I'm on it. I'll call Hector and head down there next Monday."

On his first visit, Hector showed Jourdane around the labor camps, and soon Mo began seeing clients. During the years that followed, Hector became not only Mo's interpreter and investigator but also his teacher and mentor. With Hector, Mo continued to build CRLA rapport and trust within the Soledad community that fostered the *Diana* case.

# Chapter 16
## SOLEDAD AND A PARENT STEPS FOWARD

Soledad in 1960 was a small rural farm community of about 3,000 residents planted almost smack in the center of the several miles wide Salinas Valley. "Soledad" in Spanish means "solitude," and it was an apt name for the small town nestled among the Gabilan Mountains. During the 1960s, it stretched only a mile from north to south and half a mile from east to west. Its fertile soil produced row upon row of lettuce, celery and cauliflower so far as one could see. Five miles north of town the maximum security Soledad State Prison housed some of California's most notorious prisoners. Across the Salinas River ran old Highway 101, the means of traveling between San Francisco and Los Angeles before the Interstate was opened. From March through July a considerable wind blows through the town raising dust from the adjacent fields.

On the east edge of town was the former prisoner of war camp turned into the labor camp housing several hundred families in tiny single room living quarters with a common kitchen and common toilets and showers. Aside from a few businesses and government offices, Soledad had narrow tree-lined residential streets with their small wooden homes. There were also a couple of mom-and-pop market stores, a small cantina, a four-table restaurant named Vin a Mexico, a pool hall and a small Greyhound station with its adjacent drab cafeteria where buses mostly stopped to deliver those who came to visit a husband, brother, father or son held in the nearby penitentiary.

In 1960 Soledad had two elementary schools and no high
school. The Soledad labor camp children went to the eastside
school. There were several churches including a prominent
Catholic church with a Spanish-style cathedral and parish hall
where CRLA, on Monday evenings, met those asking for help.

On a fateful day in May 1969, Elena, the mother of eleven-
year-old María, approached Hector to ask for help for her family.
The farmworker community knew that he was connected to
CRLA, and that others had asked him for assistance.

"¿En qué le puedo servir, Elena?" Hector asked what she needed.

"My daughter María wants to quit school. She says they don't
teach her anything there. It is just baby stuff in her classroom,"
she explained in Spanish.

Hector was skeptical at first. "That makes no sense. Aren't
they teaching her math and reading?"

"No, they aren't," Elena practically shouted. "They don't teach
her and the other children in the classroom anything. They just
play games. I tried to talk with María's teacher, but the teacher
does not speak Spanish. She just said that the class was 'especial,'
but it is the opposite of that."

Hector promised he would talk it over with the CRLA lawyer
and check it out with the school, "because what you say is not
what it should be for María."

Next Monday night in Soledad, Hector told Mo about his talk
with Elena.

"This does sound strange. Why don't you visit the school next
week to see what's happening with María?"

While Hector and Mo were leaving the hall of the Catholic
Church that same evening, they saw Carlos Molina waiting there
to see them.

"Good evening, Señor Jourdane. Hi, Hector, do you have a
moment to speak?"

Mo had successfully represented Molina on several minor
problems, including an occasion when the camp manager had
threatened Molina with eviction for complaining about an over-

flowing septic tank and again after Molina had complained about rent that seemed to increase almost monthly.

Molina, obviously a bit embarrassed, asked, "Would you do me the favor of coming to our home to talk? It is a private matter about my son Ramón." Molina lived with his wife and eleven children in the same labor camp Hector and his family had first lived in when they came to Soledad.

When Hector and Mo arrived at the Molina home in the labor camp, Mrs. Molina immediately sat them down to eat as Mr. Molina described the problem.

"Ramón is ten years old. He should be in the fourth grade, but the school decided he couldn't learn. The school placed Ramón in a class with twelve other children. They call it the mental retard class. All but one of the children in the class are from farmworker families."

Hector asked Molina if the children in the class were slow learners or disabled mentally.

"No. I know my son, and I know most of the other children. They might not be too smart but they are not mental retards."

Hector, remembering his conversation just a couple of days earlier, asked, "Is María in the same class as Ramón?"

"Yes, María, she is also one of the children in the class, and her mother is worried about it, just like I am."

"I remember Ramón," Mo told Molina. "He interpreted for you when you first came to see me, and one time I saw Ramón pitching for his little league baseball team. I don't understand how he could be called retarded at all."

Hector promised to check it out at the school the next day and get back to Mr. Molina.

As they left Mo said, "This is huge. This is the very case that Marty and CRLA have been looking for because this has been happening to Chicano children all over California. I'll call Marty tomorrow. He'll want to come down here."

"Okay," Hector replied. "I'll go to the school first thing tomorrow and see what they say. Then, I'll set up a meeting for you and Marty with the parents and their kids in this class. I'll get the names of any I don't know."

The next day, Hector went to María and Ramón's classroom. He looked around and could see that the class had children of all different sizes and ages. No formal instruction was going on when he arrived.

He knew the teacher, Ms. Janet Sanders. "Hi, Ms. Sanders, María's mom and Ramón's dad asked me to drop by and see how their kids were doing and what kind of class this is."

Ms. Sanders recognized him. "Oh, hi, Hector, those two are good kids, just, you know, they are slow. This is a class for the mentally retarded. They're really limited. We just try to keep them happy and help them to learn basic stuff."

Hector recognized several of the children and, by talking sympathetically with the teacher and to María and Ramón; he was able to get the names and the parents' names of all of the students.

Hector asked, "How do you know they are retarded, or slow, as you say?"

"Oh, we have intelligence tests that we give that tell us for sure about each child. See, here in my book, I have notes for each of the boys and girls in my class. So I know what they can do and learn. There are scores for each child, and they are very low."

Trying not to look too curious, Hector asked, "Can you show me?"

Ms. Sanders, pleased that Hector had taken an interest, responded, "Of course, Hector." She opened her book and pointed. "The ones on the left are what we call verbal, while on the right they are non-verbal scores."

"Thanks. This will help me explain to the parents."

He took note of each of the scores on the two parts of the IQ test for each child in the class. That information would be invaluable later on.

# Chapter 17
# MEETING IN SOLEDAD

Mo reached Marty in San Francisco the next afternoon to relay the news the Education Task Force had been waiting for: they had clients ready to challenge IQ testing. Marty was elated.

"When can you be here?" Mo asked.

"Well, I would leave right this minute . . . but check in with Hector to see when you all can arrange for a long meeting in Soledad with the parents and children. We need to do interviews to learn everything possible about who they are, how they got into the EMR classes, what they are taught . . . and everything else we'll need to bring a legal challenge."

"We're way ahead of you, boss man," Mo announced proudly. "Hector already visited the school earlier today and is arranging a meeting in Soledad with the group. I'll get right back to you with when and where."

That weekend, Marty drove to Salinas and outlined for Mo what he had learned about IQ testing. They proceeded to the Soledad parish hall, where they met with Hector and all nine of the children and their parents.

Hector arranged for Marty and Mo to speak with Ramón and his dad before the others arrived. The eleven-year-old told them he had been tested in English.

"Ramón, your mom and dad don't speak English, do they?" Mo asked.

"*No, señor.*"

"You speak English and Spanish?"

"*Sí, señor.* We talk only Spanish at home. Me and my friends, we talk only in Spanish when we're playing, but at school they no let us talk Spanish. Some of my classmates cannot talk in school the whole day because they do not speak English . . . and my English, I am still learning."

"Did the man giving the test for the special class ask whether you wanted to be tested in English or Spanish?"

"*No, señor.* He just tell me to answer the questions. I don't even know what the test is for."

"What about the other kids in your class, were they tested in Spanish?"

"I don't think so."

"Do they all speak both English and Spanish?"

"No, besides me, four do speak some English, but mostly Spanish."

"In addition to those four, do the others also speak some English too?"

"No, they speak only Spanish."

The other parents and children at the meeting confirmed Ramón's story. The children were shy at first, and translations were necessary for the parents and many of the children. Soon, the children became more outspoken about their class and their frustration with it.

Arturo, an eleven-year-old San Francisco 49er fan, spoke knowledgeably in English with Marty about John Brodie, Ken Willard, Dave Wilcox and Gene Washington—stars on the 1969 team. Arturo, impressively, could recite player statistics and call off uniform numbers of the prominent 49er players. He told the lawyers his story about how he had been tested and then dropped into the EMR class.

The other children at the meeting, with their parents, in addition to Arturo and Ramón, were Diana and her twin brother Armando, age 8; Manuel, Jr., age 10; Ernesto, age 9; María, age 11; Margarita age 12; and Rachel, age 10.

Even though this was the first meeting that both the children and most of the parents were having with any attorney, and one would expect reticence, as time went on the children seemed to be of at least normal capacity. Indeed, the parents assured Marty, Mo and Hector that their children were perfectly capable of doing chores at home and understanding complex instructions.

Hector asked Diana's mother how Diana performed at home.

She answered, "Diana does much of the cooking, most of the sewing and mending, and she does the ironing and takes good care of our younger ones."

The lawyers and Hector were noticeably impressed.

Diana's mom then relayed, "Unfortunately, our Diana misses many of her classes because, when my husband and I are out working, we need her to stay home to take care of her younger brothers and sisters."

"Did anyone at your school ask you about why you were missing days?" Hector asked Diana in Spanish.

"*No, señor. No les importa.*" They don't care.

Another mother told Hector, "Our little ones come home from school sometimes crying because the other kids call them crazy."

Manuel chimed in, "They call me 'mentally ill Manuel' and '*tonto.*'"

María's mom added, "Some of the parents in the neighborhood won't even let their children play with ours because they say our children are mentally ill or stupid."

Then Ramón told Hector, "The children in our class want to quit school because we don't learn anything there."

María repeated to Marty and Mo, "What we're given is just baby stuff."

All of the parents wanted their children taken out of the EMR class and given a chance to learn. The parents expressed their great fear that their other children, when they reached third grade, would suffer the same fate as their older brothers and sisters.

Manuel, Jr. asked Mo and Hector if they could speak with him for a minute, and they went off to an office to talk.

Manuel said, "When I was three in Greenfield, my dad was attacked by three bad men and was cut up all over, including a slash in the neck. That is why my father is disabled and unable to speak or walk very well."

"Were the men arrested?" Mo asked.

"No," the boy said, "my father refused to identify his attackers. They threatened our whole family if he talked. We moved here, where we live in a small house on Sixth Street. My mom spends all her time working and taking care of my father, so we never had time for lessons before I started school. I am a good athlete. And I got help learning English, but I was behind in class, so they gave me a big test only in English, and I did not understand it. Then they put me in the retard class."

"Did they have a translator for you?" Hector asked.

"*No, señor.* The man was an Anglo who was not friendly and he didn't seem to care much that I had trouble understanding him or the test."

The reality in Soledad that children were tested only in English added an incredible dimension to the malpractice of the school psychologists in school districts across California. It was one thing, entirely wrong in and of itself, to label a child mentally retarded based only on a biased test. It was quite another to do so based on the results of a test given in a language in which the children were not fluent.

As Hector, Marty and Mo were leaving, they thanked the parents and children for meeting with them.

María's mother looked at each of the three of them in turn and said, "If you can do something to fix this for María, you will change her whole life, and ours too."

The other parents nodded in agreement.

"Our prayers will be with you," she said.

# Chapter 18
# THE ASSOCIATION OF CHICANO PSYCHOLOGISTS

Marty and Mo returned to Salinas and discussed their game plan for the case they were going to file, not only on behalf of the Soledad families, but also as a class action suit. The CRLA would sue on behalf of every Spanish-surname child anywhere in California who had been classified as an Educable Mentally Retarded student on the basis of English-only and/or culturally biased IQ tests. Marty and Mo discussed their need for a qualified and credentialed expert school psychologist to retest the children to prove that the children were normal, not developmentally delayed at all, and to provide testimony.

At least a year earlier, Dr. Palomares had introduced Marty by phone to Dr. Steven Moreno, the President of the California Association of Chicano Psychologists, an organization which was also challenging the indiscriminate, misuse of IQ tests on Mexican-American students to place them in EMR classes. Moreno promised the organization would support litigation that challenged the status quo. Marty offered to share with Moreno and his group the findings of the other CRLA offices actively investigating EMR classes in the areas they served. He also would try to enlist interest groups, such as the Mexican American Political Association (MAPA) headed by CRLA board member Bert Corona and the Mexican American Legal Defense and Education Fund (MALDEF), founded in 1968 in Texas but also active in California.

83

Finally, he promised Moreno, "I'll touch base with Henry Der of the new group called Chinese for Affirmative Action to see if we can enlist their support."

Mo and Marty got to work on planning for the retesting of the Soledad Children so that they could meet with Soledad Unified School District officials and demand immediate changes or bring a class-action lawsuit before the beginning of the next school semester. To that end, Marty and Mo flew to San Diego to meet with Dr. Moreno in person. They asked if he could go up to Soledad to meet the children, evaluate and test them. Moreno said he would be happy to prepare an in-depth affidavit on his studies and professional conclusions to support their case. Regrettably, his fall teaching schedule and other commitments made it impossible for him to travel the 500 miles each way between San Diego and Soledad to conduct the tests and produce the written evaluations within the time CRLA needed them. He said that Dr. Palomares would likely have the same time conflicts. But, he recommended Dr. Víctor Ramírez at the Grossmont Union High School District, who was an expert psychologist that actually evaluated students on a daily basis. Moreno then called Dr. Ramírez who said he would meet with the two CRLA attorneys that day.

Shortly thereafter, Marty and Mo drove their rented Plymouth 30 miles north to Dr. Ramírez's office on Grand Street in downtown Escondido. It turned out that Ramírez was supremely qualified. Before becoming school psychologist for the Grossmont District, he was a psychologist for an elementary school district in Hawthorne, a research psychologist at Children's Hospital in Los Angeles, an intern psychologist at Metropolitan State Mental Hospital in Norwalk and a family psychologist for the YMCA in Gardena. He readily agreed to go to Soledad at his own expense and without pay to test the children and testify as needed. Ramírez explained to Marty and Mo that, "I've encountered a high percentage of Spanish-speaking students placed in the wrong class because professionals who should know better, use the number achieved on a test to justify a finding that a child has impaired learning ability. Anyone who uses tests to determine a non-mainstream child's ability to learn must be extremely cautious because the underlying premise of the test is that each child comes to the testing with the same general background and knowledge, same general range of experience and the same general range of linguistic abilities and understanding. And that simply is not true." He was adamant: "Use of a standard IQ test *alone* to determine a non-mainstream child's placement in school is *professional malpractice.* To determine the learning ability of the children you are concerned about, that is Spanish-speaking children who grew up in farm labor camps, you have to consider the child's bilingualism, cultural differences and the extensive time the child has spent out of the regular program."

Marty and Mo were delighted: CRLA had found its ideal expert.

# Chapter 19
# THE RETESTING OF THE SOLEDAD CHILDREN

On November 1, 1969, Mo drove over the Santa Cruz Mountains to the San Jose airport to pick up Dr. Ramírez and his brother who came along to help take notes on the individual meetings with the Soledad Children. During the 85-mile ride south on Highway 101 to Soledad, through the garlic fields and cherry orchards surrounding Gilroy and the Prunedale apple orchards, the psychologist explained to Mo, "Even though my family spoke Spanish and I learned it from them, it is not simple, even for me, to measure the intelligence of children who grow up in a farm labor camp. And, this problem is not limited to rural California and Mexicans. An African American professional, especially one not schooled in the culture and vocabulary of African American youth growing up in South Central Los Angeles, will likely not understand or be able to appreciate and measure the child's background, colloquial language or prior learning opportunities. A child in a labor camp or a city ghetto who is known to his peers as a smart and talented leader may nevertheless struggle in a testing environment. So, unless one is open and sensitive to that culture, any diagnosis may be in serious error."

And then Ramírez made a startling further explanation of harm from improper testing: "Labeling a child mentally retarded can lead to the child fulfilling that expectation."

"Meaning?" Mo asked.

"If you tell a little girl she's mentally retarded," he explained, "and treat her as retarded, the young lady will view herself and present as one of lower than normal capacity. Had the same girl been told from birth that she was gifted and been treated as gifted, she might well attend Stanford."

Hector had arranged with all of the parents and the children for the retesting over the weekend of November 1 and November 2, 1969. Hector had explained to the Soledad parents that the retesting could prove that the children did not belong in the "retarded" classroom.

Dr. Ramírez evaluated the nine children that the Soledad Elementary School District had placed in the class for the mentally retarded. He obtained specific information about each child and his or her family, and he gave each child a wide range of achievement tests to determine the language in which the child was proficient, as well as their level of proficiency in reading, math and spelling. Ramírez subsequently gave each child the WISC IQ test in Spanish or English without varying or eliminating any question on the test. He gave each child the opportunity to respond in either language or a combination of both languages.

The children understood fully what was going on. They were eager to do well and pleased to be able to talk to a tester who understood and cared about them. After his two days with the children and after he had gone home and had time to organize his notes, Dr. Ramírez relayed his test results and preliminary conclusions.

"Really good news," he said. "The average gain of the group on the retest was an entire standard deviation." While not surprised, the lawyers were elated with the results.

"Fantastic!" exclaimed Mo.

"The previous tests of the children by the Soledad Elementary School district psychologists," he went on, "had ranged from 30 to 72 with a mean score of $63^{1}/_{2}$, well below the 70 Weschler test cutoff for EMR class placement. On the retest, their scores ranged from 67 to 89 with a mean of 76. Significantly, every child scored on the non-verbal section of the test at a level above the Soledad EMR class assignment standard, achieving a mean score of 86 on the non-verbal section of the tests."

"Thank you so much for your dedicated work, Víctor," Marty said. "We'll be able to go after this well-armed now."

Ramírez promised to send them his more detailed report as soon as he could and said, "Seven of the nine children I tested are clearly not in the right classroom. I'm not as sure about the other two, given their overall test results."

"Don't the test scores of the two in question have to be adjusted for their years in a class with virtually no instruction, for the cultural bias in the test instrument itself and for the fact that, despite these limitations both children tested in the normal range on the non-verbal parts of the test?" Marty asked.

"You know," Ramírez began, "you're totally right about that. Given those facts and their scores, it really is the case that all nine should exit that class as soon as possible. The key now is that all should be provided a carefully designed transition program into regular class settings, with special care given to the youngest ones."

Besides being the correct conclusion in the view of the lawyers, the recommendation to remove all nine from EMR made unnecessary what would have been a devastating discussion with the parents of any child left behind. Mo and Marty called Hector, who relayed the good news to the families anxiously waiting to learn the results.

# Chapter 20
## RETEST RESULTS IN DETAIL

Arturo scored a 94 on the verbal portion of the exam and an 86 on the non-verbal portion, for a full-scale Weschler IQ of 89. The wide-range achievement test reflected Arturo's reading and spelling levels at grade 1.9 and grade 3.2 in arithmetic. Thus, even with a reading and spelling proficiency more than two years behind his grade level, Arturo had scored not far below average for his age level and more than 20 points higher than the results previously obtained by the district that placed him in classes for the Educable Mentally Retarded.

Dr. Ramírez concluded that, "Arthur is far more capable academically and socially than his present school placement would indicate. Arthur is capable of functioning within a regular school program and should be allowed the opportunity to succeed at that level."

Eight-year-old Diana scored a 67 on the verbal portion of the exam but a 96 on the non-verbal portion, for a full-scale IQ of 79. Her achievement test reflected Diana's reading level and her math level at pre-kindergarten. Indeed, Diana had not yet learned the alphabet nor had she been taught rudimentary numbers skills. This accounted for her previous score of 30 on the verbal Stanford-Binet test she was given. Her non-verbal score completely disproved "retardation." Dr. Ramírez gave Diana another recognized test to evaluate verbal ability and scholastic aptitude called the Peabody Picture Vocabulary test, and she scored much higher still. Ramírez believed a neurologic exam for Diana would be appropriate, but in any case, she was certainly not mentally impaired.

Only months after his father had come forward to talk with Mo, ten-year-old Manuel scored an 82 on the verbal portion of the exam and an 86 on the non-verbal portion, for a total IQ score of 84. This was a score more than 15 points higher than his previous result and well outside the EMR range. His achievement test reflected Manuel at grade 1.9 in reading and grade 2.6 in arithmetic. Some three years after he had been placed in the EMR class, Ramírez concluded that Manuel should have been in a regular classroom all along.

Nine-year-old Ernesto scored a 71 on the verbal portion of the exam and a 92 on the non-verbal portion, for a total IQ of 79. The achievement test found Ernesto's reading level to be that of a kindergartner, but he was not performing far below his grade level in math. As with every one of the children tested, Ernesto's IQ score had increased significantly in the retest.

Eleven-year-old María scored a 74 on the verbal portion of the exam and an 87 on the non-verbal portion, for a total IQ of 78, despite reading more than two years below her grade level.

Ten-year-old Ramón scored an 81 on the verbal portion of the exam and a 75 on the non-verbal portion. The achievement test reflected that Ramón's was reading at a grade level of 2.3 and in arithmetic at a 3.6, indicating that he had managed to progress remarkably despite the obstacles his lack of school instruction represented.

Armando scored a 77 on the verbal portion of the exam and a 72 on the non-verbal portion. His achievement test results were the same as those of his twin sister, Diana. Despite the fact that he did not speak or read in English, his verbal score was well above the EMR cut-off score.

Twelve-year-old Margarita, who by that age should have been in seventh grade, scored a 62 on the verbal portion of the exam but an 83 on the non-verbal portion, for a full-scale IQ of 76, a score achieved despite the fact that she was being compared to other children in the seventh grade who had the benefit of regular schooling. Her achievement test reflected she was reading at only a grade level of 1.7 and in arithmetic at a level of 3.4.

Finally, eleven-year-old Rachel scored a 66 on the verbal portion of the exam and a 74 on the non-verbal portion. Her achievement test reflected she was reading at a level of 1.5 and in arithmetic at a level of 2.6. Dr. Ramírez had first noted that this result might support a possible diagnosis of borderline retardation, but, on further analysis, he said it was noteworthy that Rachel's lowest scores were in the areas of social assimilation and information related to Anglo culture. He pointed out that she had an excessive number of absences from school, due to family problems she had encountered, which had also contributed to her low scores. Thus, he recommended that she too should be removed from EMR placement so long as she was given extra help.

Dr. Ramírez provided his final written evaluation and recommendation for each child on December 18, 1969, but authorized CRLA to work with a draft of his report a few days earlier, because time was of the essence.

It was time to meet with the district.

# Chapter 21
## CRUZ REYNOSO

Cruz Reynoso was the first chairman of the board of CRLA. He was as important to its ultimate success as its founder Jim Lorenz. After a year as CRLA chairman, he relinquished that position and moved to Washington DC to become Associate General Counsel for the Equal Employment Opportunity Commission (EEOC). In 1968, Cruz returned to California to become the second Executive Director of CRLA. Cruz was a magnetic and determined leader with extensive leadership experience and skills.

Cruz was born in Brea, Orange County, California. He and his ten siblings picked oranges in the Southern California groves when they were young. When Cruz was seven, his family moved to a barrio in La Habra, where he first attended an all-Latino elementary school and then the fully integrated Fullerton High School. He received an Associate of Arts degree from Fullerton College in 1951 and then enrolled at Pomona College on a scholarship, graduating with a B. A. in 1953. Cruz joined the Army after graduation and served in the Counterintelligence Corps for two years. He graduated from law school at the University of California-Berkeley in 1958 and spent two years after graduation at the National University of Mexico. Cruz and a partner established a law office in El Centro in 1960 and practiced there until he joined the EEOC in Washington DC.

In early 1968, Jim Lorenz met with Marty, Bob and Mickey Bennett, the CRLA chief administrator, to announce that he thought it was time to find his successor. Jim wished to spend more time on a CRLA lawsuit against the University of California at Davis he was passionately interested in, a case challenging the massive sums devoted to the mechanization of agriculture in California with virtually no resources devoted to transition training for the displaced farmworkers. Jim also thought it was time to distance himself from the day-to-day administration of the ten CRLA offices.

They immediately thought of Cruz Reynoso for Jim's replacement. Marty and Mickey Bennett set up an appointment to meet Cruz in Washington DC. Of course, Reynoso already knew a great deal about CRLA, but he asked many questions, ranging from the subject of funding to personnel and, particularly, the program's litigation priorities. At the conclusion of the interview, he said he was quite interested and would talk it over with his wife Jeannene and get back to them. A week later Cruz called and said that, for family reasons, his next move needed to be back to the San Francisco Bay Area. He gladly would accept the job and the challenge that came with it, if he could be located there.

The CRLA leadership had already discussed that Los Angeles was not central to most CRLA offices. It did not take long for the CRLA leadership to decide to move the central office to San Francisco and for Bob and Marty to move there in order to better coordinate the program. Animated discussion of titles for the group resulted in denominating Jim as Chief Deputy Director of "Operations" and Bob as Chief Deputy Director of "Organization." Marty became Director of Litigation and later, when Sheldon Greene joined them in San Francisco, he assumed the title of General Counsel. CRLA moved at the end of 1968, and Cruz was appointed initially as a Deputy Director, at his request, to get oriented for a few months before he formally assumed the leadership of the program.

Cruz had a very strong and abiding interest in education and was a regular participant in the Education Task Force meetings. Marty and Mo suggested it might add weight if Cruz joined them in meeting with the Soledad School District representatives. Cruz replied that they would not be able to keep him away from such a meeting if they tried.

# Chapter 22
# MEETINGS WITH SOLEDAD OFFICIALS

Mo contacted the Soledad school superintendent, Wendell Broom, and a meeting was set for December 15, 1969, in Soledad. The three CRLA lawyers and Hector were greeted with an offer of coffee and then escorted into the superintendent's office, where they settled into the lone visitor's chair and the three folding chairs that were brought in for the occasion.

The affidavit that Cruz Reynoso later filed in court in support of CRLA's request for a temporary and preliminary injunction summarized the meeting as well as developments after the meeting:

> AFFIDAVIT OF CRUZ REYNOSO
> STATE OF CALIFORNIA
> COUNTY OF SAN FRANCISCO
> I, CRUZ REYNOSO, being duly sworn, hereby depose and say:
>
> I am the Executive Director of California Rural Legal Assistance and a member of the State Bar of California. On December 15, 1969, attorneys Martin Glick, Maurice Jourdane, and I met with Soledad Elementary School Superintendent Wendell Broom to review the facts we had uncovered in our investigation of placement of Mexican-American school children in classes for the mentally retarded in Soledad and throughout the State of California. All of the allegations in the complaint filed in this action were discussed with Mr. Broom — including (1) the high IQ scores on the retest, (2) the statewide pattern of discriminatory placement of the Spanish-speaking in classes with the gen-

uinely mentally retarded, and (3) the great harm being caused and urgency of quick action were discussed with him. Two days thereafter complete copies of the test results and recommendations obtained by bilingual psychologist, Victor Ramírez, were provided to the Superintendent.

Mr. Broom asserted that he had previously suspected that unfair testing of Mexican Americans had occurred because they were tested in English. He unequivocally assured us that he could reassign the children immediately after Christmas vacation to regular classes and that he could use existing facilities for high powered supplementary training in language and mathematics to correct past deficiencies caused by their improper placement so that the children would be fully integrated into the normal program as quickly as possible.

Mr. Broom stated that the Christmas vacation provided the most opportune time for this transition as the school would devise a schedule during this period and the children in the school would accept the change as a natural one. He further assured plaintiffs that the tests already administered to the children would be sufficient so long as the psychologist who administered them was certified by the State of California.

On December 30, 1969, 15 days after the school officials had promised to re-assign the children, an agent of the school district sent a letter to the parents changing the school's position, adding that a "complete study" would be necessary and asking for further documentation. In spite of plaintiff's warnings, in response, that any further delay in providing the children with a regular education would endanger their chances to make up for the three years of deprivation already suffered, the children upon return from Christmas vacation on January 5, 1970, were and are presently forced to stay in the class for mentally retarded.

Cruz Reynoso

As Cruz recited in his affidavit, the meeting in mid-December with Superintendent Broom seemed like a home run for the CRLA clients because he was very receptive to the facts laid out and the proposed short-term solution. Broom's statement that he had "always wondered" about testing children in a language they did not speak was one that memory has not dimmed some fifty years later, but the CRLA lawyers did not interrogate him on the matter.

Broom's quick assurances that the Soledad District would do all that CRLA lawyers had suggested was, in fact, bittersweet. It was terrific for Diana, María, Ramón, Arturo and the other children and their families. When CRLA lawyers told the parents that the district had agreed to take all of the Soledad Children out of the EMR class and provide help to ease their transition into the regular classroom, they were overjoyed. The downside was that the agreed settlement would make the Soledad group, no longer in EMR classes, at least arguably improper as named plaintiffs able to represent the statewide class of the other 13,000 wrongfully placed Mexican-American children. Thus, the lawsuit would have to wait until CRLA located other improperly placed children as plaintiffs and retested them. Mo, Marty and Cruz were thrilled for their clients and they told each other that all of the work they had done getting the legal papers ready to go would still be ultimately useful.

When the district sent its letter two weeks later, completely reneging on its promises, work around the clock commenced to file the *Diana* case the first week of January.

On Monday, January 5, 1970, in a last attempt to get the Soledad Children out of the EMR class at the beginning of the year, Cruz, Marty and Mo met in Salinas with the two Monterey County psychologists who did the testing for the county school districts, including Soledad. The psychologists were defensive and antagonistic. They showed no regret for conducting IQ testing in a language other than the primary one understood by their test subjects, nor did they even try to excuse their failure to use a translator. They were openly critical of Dr. Ramírez and said it was "unethical" for CRLA to have brought an unsupervised, outside tester into their territory.

One of the county psychologists proudly and defiantly turned to Marty and said, "You know, I once tested an eight-year-old boy who spoke only Latvian, and I know no Latvian at all, but I had no trouble showing that young man where to make marks on his test paper, and I know I assessed him accurately."

Dumbfounded, Marty refrained from asking if the results from the test of the Latvian boy determined him to be among the least intelligent this psychologist had ever encountered. Instead, he asked if the two Monterey County professionals could at least support a reassignment to see how the children responded. They refused.

One of them said, "We could maybe do our own retest, but that will take a while because we have several other third graders to test this semester, and your clients would need to go to the back of that line."

A school board meeting was set for later that day. It became clear at the meeting that the refusal to make an immediate change was set in stone. Settlement with the Soledad Unified School District was now a dead issue and the class action was a go. *Diana v. State Board of Education* was filed on Marty's 30th birthday, January 7, 1970.

Armando Menocal, 2019. Courtesy of Laura Rodriguez (Armando's wife).

Clair Burgener, 1973. Used with permission of the Collection of the U.S. House of Representatives.

Dr. Uvaldo Palomares,
2019. Courtesy of Uvaldo
Palomares, Jr. (his son).

Cruz Reynoso, 2018.
Courtesy of Marty Glick.

Ramón Racio, Marty Glick, Maurice Jourdane, 2005. Courtesy of Hector de la Rosa.

Hector de la Rosa, César Chávez, Henry Cantú, 1970. Courtesy of former CRLA attorney W.B. Daniels.

Manuel Reyes, 2019. Self-photograph.

Marty Glick, 1970. Courtesy of former CRLA attorney W.B. Daniels.

Maurice Jourdane, 1972. Courtesy of Mo Jourdane, passport photo.

Soledad EMR class, 1969. From left to right, bottom row: #2 Arturo, #3 Ramón, #4 Rachel, #5 Diana, #8 Manuel; top row: #1 Armando, #2 Margarita, #4 María. Courtesy of Manuel Reyes.

Judge Robert Peckham (Swearing In), 1966. Courtesy of Palo Alto Historical Society.

Soledad labor camp, 1970. Courtesy of former CRLA attorney W.B. Daniels.

THE VICE PRESIDENT

WASHINGTON

September 16, 1968

Dear Mr. Glick:

Thank you for your letter concerning your office's representation of the California farmworkers.

I asked my staff to look into the matters discussed in your letter. They checked with the Department of Labor and have been informed that Mr. Robert C. Goodwin, Administrator of the Bureau of Employment Security, responded to your letter for Secretary Wirtz on September 6. I have been told that the circumstances stated in that letter have not changed. There are no formal requests by the growers now pending before the Department of Labor.

I also understand that your office met with Mr. Glenn E. Brockway, the Regional Administrator of the Bureau of Employment Security for that area, to discuss the charges made in your letter. I am sure that appropriate action will be taken to resolve these matters.

Again, thank you for bringing these matters to my attention.

Sincerely,

Hubert H. Humphrey

Mr. Martin R. Glick
Attorney
California Rural Legal Assistance
711 South Main Street
Salinas, California 93901

Letter from Hubert Humphrey to Marty Glick, 9-16-68. Courtesy of Marty Glick.

## THE WALL STREET JOURNAL.

### Court Orders Tests of IQ In Pupils' Home Languages

*By a* WALL STREET JOURNAL *Staff Reporter*

SAN FRANCISCO — California school children whose language at home is other than English must be tested in both their primary language and in English before they can be placed in classes for the mentally retarded, according to a settlement reached in Federal district court here.

The settlement between state education officials and California Rural Legal Assistance, an antipoverty agency, was made in response to a suit filed by the agency last Jan. 7. The suit was brought on behalf of nine Mexican-American children who, the agency argued, were put in classes for the mentally retarded after they were given IQ, or intelligence, tests in English.

The settlement also provides that Mexican-American and Chinese children already in classes for mentally retarded must be retested in their primary language, unless they were previously tested in it.

Wall Street Journal article on Diana case victory, 2-9-70. Courtesy of *Wall Street Journal*.

"Out here in the West, FIRST we have the hanging, THEN the trial!"

*LA Times* cartoon by Paul F. Conrad, 4-29-71. Used with permission of the Conrad Estate. "Out here in the West, FIRST we have the hanging, THEN the trial!"

# Chapter 23
## THE *DIANA* COMPLAINT

In mainstream legal practice, a complaint is just a pleading that, in a bare bones fashion, sets forth who the parties are, enough facts to identify the issues and a statement of the cause (or causes) of action, e.g. breach of contract or product liability or fraud. Since factual allegations made in a pleading are binding on the party making them, the prevailing wisdom has most often been that less is more. CRLA had a very different strategy.

Marty and Bob were concerned that judges would be skeptical of claims filed by CRLA that were not substantiated with a compelling statement of facts. Additionally, they knew that the press would be more likely to feature their litigation when the complaint provided real color. Even in rural California, the press could be a powerful ally, bringing public attention to the practices and action that the target of litigation, in this case the Soledad Unified School District, would prefer not be made public.

Thus, the "speaking" complaint became *de rigueur* at CRLA. A "speaking complaint" is one loaded with facts that add color and highlight and bring into clear focus the alleged abuse. Marty and Mo poured into the *Diana* complaint the findings of all the research done by the Education Task Force; the data accumulated, the compelling facts of the injustice to Rachel, Manuel, Margarita, Armando, Diana, Arturo, María, Ernesto and Ramón, and the results of the retesting. It read much more like a novel than a court document.

The complaint also reflected the weeks Marty and Mo had spent strategizing with other attorneys and experts inside and outside of CRLA, as wells as with the parents of the Soledad children. They had to decide where to file the case to get the best possible judge assigned to it. They also deliberated on which individuals and entities they should sue, whether or not there should be other plaintiffs and, most critically, exactly what remedy or remedies should be sought and when to seek them. It was imperative to think through very carefully how a new system would operate for EMR placement if IQ tests were eliminated.

# Chapter 24
# JUDGE ASSIGNMENT

That Supreme Court Justices Ruth Bader Ginsburg and Clarence Thomas see the issues through a different lens from each other and some of the other Supreme Court Justices has been documented in their decisions and in their public statements. Indeed, social and ideological issues have divided the Supreme Court of the United States for decades, often leaving outcomes on that court to the swing vote of one or two justices. Such differences are hardly limited to judges on the highest court in the land. Judges at all levels come to their positions from radically different backgrounds; they have different life experiences, temperaments and opinions. For CRLA and the clients it represented, the judge that would be assigned to their case was going to be an important variable.

Marty and Bob, soon after their arrival in Salinas, studied just how judges were assigned to cases filed in the Northern District of California. When *Diana* was filed at the beginning of 1970, there were sharp differences in the Northern District panel, with more progressive judges Alphonso Zirpoli, Albert Wollenberg, Stanley Weigel and Robert Peckham in one wing and ultra-conservative and often impatient judges Howard Schnacke, Lloyd Burke and Samuel Conti in the other wing. Judge Oliver Carter was viewed as more middle-of-the-road but very slow to make decisions, and Judge William Sweigert was viewed as neutral but a bit right of center.

Glick and Gnaizda personally visited the office of the Clerk of the Court on the 16th floor of the San Francisco Federal Building on Golden Gate Avenue. There they observed that the judges' names were on slips of paper inserted into wheels that the clerks would spin with the draw taken from the bottom part of the wheel when it came to a stop. They talked with an amiable court clerk and learned that they distributed the various categories of cases among the judges as equally as possible: civil rights, labor and employment, torts, etc. Depending upon recent assignments, some judges' names would be included in the spin for cases falling into a particular category at any given time. They also learned that the clerks restocked the wheels twice a year.

The clerk told Marty and Bob, "The filing party is responsible for putting the appropriate category on the cover page."

After learning the mechanics of the system, Marty and Bob had the CRLA staff review and tally by category all Northern District court filings during the previous six months. Then, Marty carefully tracked and recorded the names of every Northern District judge drawn by category so CRLA could increase its odds of a better draw in a particular week or in a particular category. Many cases could be reasonably denominated to be in two or three different categories, and that gave them some flexibility to increase the odds of a favorable draw. With one politically sensitive case where Marty and Bob were concerned that a bad draw could doom their clients, they concocted a scheme for Marty to file and watch the draw from the wheel while Bob waited, hopefully out of sight, in the doorway of the Clerk of the Court's office. If the draw was unfortunate, Marty was to drop his briefcase to the floor to create a distraction and make a loud noise before the judge's name drawn would be stamped on the pleading by the clerk. Upon hearing the bang of the briefcase, Bob was to rush in and proclaim that they had made a mistake on the category listed on the pleading to see if they could get the clerk to do a new draw from a different wheel before it was too late. It was a crazy scheme that, fortunately, they were never compelled to test, because the draw in that particular case ended up being a favorable one. But in the Diana case, the draw did not go in their favor.

As it happened, Judge Lloyd Burke was the name drawn and stamped on the complaint. Judge Burke was about the worst draw possible. A former attorney general and a distinguished sergeant in World War II, Burke was abrupt and decidedly to the far right on social issues.

There was an alternative, however. There existed a San Jose division of the Northern District of California. The San Jose outpost added a special opportunity for litigation, as counsel could apply to have cases reassigned to the San Jose division, if that were "more convenient." Thus, for the CRLA offices in Gilroy, Salinas and Soledad, San Jose was *always* "more convenient." In connection with the filing of the *Diana* case, Marty and Mo prepared the required form to request a convenience re-assignment to San Jose.

To put it mildly, the CRLA lawyers breathed a sigh of deep relief when, on January 8, both Judges Burke and Peckham signed their names to a form approving the transfer, and then acting Chief Judge Albert Wollenberg signed the order granting their geographic convenience request to transfer *Diana v. State Board of Education*, Civil No. C-70-37-RFP, to Judge Peckham.

Judge Robert Francis Peckham was one of the most respected judges to ever serve in the Northern District of California, (geographically, a very large district that stretched north to the Oregon border, east to Vacaville and south to San Luis Obispo). Peckham was a graduate of Yale University and the Stanford Law School. He had worked in private practice for many years and had been an attorney with the US Attorney's office in San Francisco from 1948 to 1953. He had also served on the Santa Clara Superior Court from 1959 to 1966, when Lyndon Johnson appointed him to a newly created seat on the Northern District panel. Throughout his career on the bench, Judge Peckham gained praise as a very fair and diligent judge who worked hard to make correct decisions. He was always courteous to litigants, jurors and counsel and was compassionate about rendering justice. Despite his seemingly inbred courtesy and kindly ways, he enforced his rules, and there was never any doubt in his courtroom about who was in charge.

# Chapter 25
# THE PLAINTIFFS AND THE DEFENDANTS IDENTIFIED

Of course, the plaintiffs and class representatives would include the nine Soledad children with their parents as *guardians ad litem* (i.e., for the litigation) on their behalf, but Marty and Mo decided to add a second group: José, Angie, Manuela, Lucía and Andrés, Jr. As the complaint filed ultimately stated,

> The second group of plaintiffs are other children of the same families with the same language and culture background. Some are preschoolers about to enter school and the others are now in first and second grade and are about to be given IQ tests. All fear that the system will inevitably lead to their placement in a class for the mentally retarded. . . . Lucía 10, [was] told by school officials she might be placed in an EMR class.

Adding the younger children was important so that their fate, and the fate of similar children in the hundreds of other California school districts, would be addressed in any settlement or litigated outcome. It also gave the story a greater scope, by establishing that the case was about protecting future generations as well as trying to save those students who had already been placed in the EMR classes. Finally, having this additional group made it much more difficult for the defendants to attempt to moot the case by providing quick relief for the nine and ignore the rest of the class of hundreds of thousands who might end up in the dead-end classes.

To protect the children and parents from invasion of their privacy, Marty, at the time of filing of the complaint, also filed a formal written request for a protective order blacking out all plaintiff family last names. Judge Peckham signed that order on January 8, 1970.

At the local level, the decision was to sue the Soledad Unified School District and all members of the district board by name. They were appropriate defendants because their passivity had allowed the insidious practice of placing a disproportionate number of Spanish-speaking children into EMR classes to continue. Adding them by name therefore put pressure to step up to their responsibilities. CRLA named the Soledad Unified School District Superintendent Broom, the lead local official. At the State of California level, the defendants were the State Board of Education and its individual members (named individually, as were the Soledad individuals). Also added as defendants were the responsible state elected officials: Superintendent of Public Instruction Max Rafferty, State Comptroller Houston Flournoy and State Treasurer Ivy Baker Priest. Rafferty was the lead state official responsible for public education. It was necessary to name Flournoy and Priest as defendants because the complainants sought funds to pay for supplemental aid for transitioning students.

# Chapter 26
# THE REMEDY ISSUE

For the Soledad Children, CRLA sought immediate accept-
ance of the results and recommendations made in the Víctor
Ramírez testing or, if the defendants could put forth "substantial
grounds for objection to the validity of the [Ramírez] tests,"
immediate retests of the nine by a qualified bilingual tester. The
complaint also sought immediate placement into regular classrooms with "intensive supplemental training in language and
mathematics to allow them to achieve parity with their peers as
soon as possible" and removal from their school records of "any
and all indications that these children were or are mentally retarded or in a class for the mentally retarded."

As to the class of statewide children, Marty and Mo were very
confident that CRLA would prove conclusively that the IQ tests
were invalid as a test for mental retardation of culturally different
children, even when administered in the language of the test taker
by someone fluent in English and in the pupil's primary language.
Simply demanding that the State outlaw all use of the IQ tests then
existing was an obvious option. But, mindful of the old and wise
adage, "Be careful what you wish for," the idea of IQ test abolition
was soon rejected. Marty and Mo, along with the Chicano psychologists working with them feared that if IQ tests were simply abol-
ished and nothing took their place, local school districts that had
been placing kids in EMR based on a test they could not read
would continue to send them there unfettered and in even greater
numbers if there were no test at all. They reasoned that the IQ tests
with all their flaws could be effectively used as a critical

*barrier* to placement of a child in an EMR class who did not belong there. Thus they decided to ask for a mandate that would continue the use of the Weschler IQ test, administered in the primary home language of each child, but that only the non-verbal section of the test could be given, the part of the test on which the Soledad Children had performed so much better. That section, made up of mostly numbers, graphs and pictures, was significantly less culturally biased. Also part of the remedy they planned to request was to preclude districts from assigning a child to EMR classes if that child scored at or better than two standard deviations from the norm, a score of 70, on just the non-verbal section of the Weschler. This ironclad restriction was necessary and important because some districts were using a score of 85 instead of 70 on the Weschler—only one standard deviation—as the result below which they could freely classify children as retarded in spite of the fact that there wasn't the slightest scientific justification for this practice. Continued use of the non-verbal section was to be sought as an interim solution until the development of an entirely new IQ test, a so-called "culturally fair" IQ test, which would eliminate obviously unfair items and would be formulated for Mexican-American children. Both the experts assisting Marty and Mo and those working for the California Department of Education said that the development of this new test would take several years.

Víctor Ramírez and Steve Moreno initially expressed their concern that the WISC was not necessarily reliable if only half of it, the non-verbal section, were to be used.

Mo responded without hesitation. "So what?"

Marty added, "They've been misused for years, so let's employ them now in a way that will actually be fair and helpful."

Both Ramírez and Moreno agreed they would fully endorse that remedy as an interim solution.

The complaint further sought retesting of every bilingual and Spanish-speaking child in EMR classes statewide. It also called for an order to forbid assignment of any child to an EMR class unless tested in their predominant language (and with a non-verbal score at or below two standard deviations). The complaint called for a "newly developed test properly standardized by culture in Spanish and English and constructed to reflect cultural values of the Mexican American."

Finally, to be able to monitor compliance with any court orders that were issued, CRLA would have to be sent a copy of the relevant data not just by county for the 58 counties in California, but also, and more importantly, for each of the 1,300 individual school districts that enrolled students in EMR classes.

# Chapter 27
## THE COMPLAINT TELLS THE WHOLE STORY

Eric Brazil was a reporter for the *Salinas Californian* and the son of Monterey County Superior Court Judge Anthony Brazil. Eric covered CRLA regularly, and Marty and Bob had cultivated a good relationship with him. He respected the confidentiality imposed before cases became public and called his own shots entirely on how he would cover and report on the stories he authored.

When Marty met with Eric in late 1969 to describe the IQ test challenge, Eric knew it was a major story. Before filing the complaint in 1970, Marty gave Eric an advance copy, and he prepared to run it in the *Californian* and submit it to the wire services so it would circulate more broadly. It was critical therefore for both the court and the media that the complaint be compelling. It was more than that. Some of the most impactful parts of the complaint read as follows:

1. The State of California authorizes separate classes for mentally retarded children. These classes provide children minimal training in reading, spelling and math. They also teach children "body care and cleanliness, how to slice meat, how to fold a piece of paper diagonally and how to chew and swallow food." Section 690 of the California Education Code states that each class should be designed "to make them [the children] economically useful and socially adjusted."

2. Placement in one of these classes has been tantamount to a life sentence of illiteracy and public dependency. The stig-

ma that attaches from such a placement causes ridicule from other children and produces a profound sense of inferiority and shame in the child. It is therefore of paramount importance that no child be placed in such a class unless it is clear beyond reasonable doubt that he suffers from an impairment of ability to learn.

3. Between the ages of four and eight a number of school children are individually given an "IQ" test supposedly designed to measure their intellectual ability. Generally, either the Stanford-Binet or Weschler ("WISC") test is given and in most California counties the tests are given only in English. In Monterey County School Districts a child with a score of 70-55 on the WISC test or 68-52 on the Stanford-Binet will be placed in an EMR (educable mentally retarded) class. Most school districts in California use this same scale as a basis for placement of elementary school children in EMR classes. On the basis of such tests, each of the plaintiffs was placed in an EMR class.

4. The IQ scores of the nine plaintiffs when tested solely in English by a non-Spanish-speaking tester ranged from 30 to 72 with a mean score of 63 1/2. On November 1 and 2, 1969, each of the nine was individually retested by an accredited California School psychologist. Each was given the WISC test (in English and/or Spanish) and each was permitted to respond in either language. Seven of the nine scored *higher* than the *maximum* score used by the county as the ceiling for mentally retarded. These seven ranged from 2 to 19 points above the maximum with an average of 8½ points over the cut-off. One of the other two scored right on the line and the ninth student was three points below.

5. Diana improved 49 points over an earlier Stanford-Binet test. Her brother Armando jumped 22 points. Three other children showed very substantial gains of 20, 14 and 10 points. The average gain was 15 points.

6. The IQ test is a comparison of children at the same age levels. Thus Arturo, age 11 years and 2 months, is compared with all other school children aged 11 years, 2 months, to

compute his mental ability. But one does not intuit arithmetic. He [or she] must be taught multiplication and world history and geography to be able to answer questions about them. The whole notion that children should be compared to others in their own age group is based on the assumption that such children will have had similar exposure to learning, not only on the physiological growth or expansion of their brain.

7. The plaintiff children in Soledad range in age from 8 to 13 years, yet they are all taught together in one room, Room 15 of the Soledad Elementary School. They are sometimes divided into two groups for teaching, but that is the extent of differential treatment. Since there is only one teacher for the class, the two groups are taught simultaneously. The children spend substantial class time coloring in coloring books and cutting pictures out of magazines. Eleven-year-old Maria characterized the classroom activities as "baby stuff." One of the younger children cries frequently, making teaching in the class very difficult. While Arturo and the other plaintiffs in their EMR class receive this limited education, 98% of the school children the same age as Arturo have had years of formal school training. If the recent WISC tests taken by the nine plaintiffs had been compared with scores achieved by children two years younger and thus exposed to roughly the same opportunity to learn, the IQ's of the nine would be 108, 107, 101, 99, 94, 98, 91, 89 and 81.

8. Because of the widely dissimilar exposure to learning offered to children from low-income and minority families, it is well documented that IQ score has no relation to the ability of such children to learn. Alfred Binet, creator of the IQ test, points out: "Some recent philosophers appear to have given their moral support to the deplorable verdict that the intelligence of an individual is a fixed quantity . . . we must protest. . . . A child's mind is like a field for which an expert farmer has advised a change in the method of cultivating, with the result that in the place of desert land, we now have a harvest."

9. The Weschler (WISC) test is divided into two parts labeled (1) "Verbal" and (2) "Non-verbal." The "verbal" part contains the vocabulary, general information, story problem arithmetic, word similarities and general comprehension sections. The "non-verbal" part, by contrast, requires only enough verbal skill to understand test directions. The non-verbal sections require children to complete pictures, use codes, arrange pictures in the right order, assemble objects and use blocks to make designs. The results of the nine plaintiffs on the two sections show clearly the impact culture and language have on their ability to perform well on the test. On the verbal IQ scale, their mean score is 75 and the median score is 74. Their non-verbal IQ scale shows a score that averages 10-11 points higher with a mean of 84 and a median of 86. Margarita had a verbal IQ score of 62 and a non-verbal IQ of 83. Diana scores only 67 on the verbal IQ section but shows a non-verbal IQ of 96. Since Diana at age 8$^1$/2 has never even been taught the alphabet, it is no wonder that she cannot cope with the verbal sections of the test. Her situation is not unique. Achievement tests given to these children show that 8 of the 9 are only at first-grade level or lower in both reading and spelling. *None* of the children has a *non-verbal* IQ below the maximum ceiling for mental retardation used in Monterey County and only 3 have scores in the 70s.

10. The Stanford-Binet test, by contrast to the WISC test, is 100% verbal. Plaintiff Diana was tested in English only when she was given the Stanford-Binet by Monterey County testers and scored an IQ of 30. Even though this result is patently absurd—persons with IQ that low cannot physically care for themselves—no note of the possible cause of this score was made on her record.

11. A few sample test questions will suffice to show the problem that the Mexican-American, rural child encounters. The *General Information* section of one of the IQ tests includes: "Who wrote Romeo and Juliet?" and "When is

Labor Day?" It asks, "What is the color of rubies?" instead
of "What is the color of plums?" The *General Comprehension* section includes questions that ask, "Why is it better
to pay bills by check than by cash?"—a very difficult question for a child whose parents never had a bank account.
The *vocabulary* section asks about "umbrella" not "som-
brero," "microscope" not "magnifying glass" and "chattel"
not "slave." The test also asks children to identify
"C.O.D.," "hieroglyphic" and "Genghis Khan."

12. The most important source of knowledge for the child,
particularly the pre-schooler, is his or her parents. Parents
obviously can't teach more than they know. In the Mexican-American home, the information that is forthcoming
will be in Spanish and will be more likely to relate to Mexico and Mexican cultural values than to the United States
and its values and laws. The middle-class parent spends
time with his or her children teaching what psychologists
have termed the "hidden curriculum." Thus, the middle-
class Anglo-American child is intensively tutored by his
parents, including correction of speech, grammar, syntax
and style while his Mexican-American counterpart has not
yet been exposed to the language. Therefore, any test relating to verbal skills is totally invalid as any indication of the
learning ability of such Mexican-American children.

13. The farmworker's child grows up without awareness of or
experience with books, pictures or magazines. There is a
paucity of objects in his home. Of course, a child cannot
identify what he has never encountered. Rarely has a Mexican-American child from Soledad been further from
home than Salinas, the major town in the county some 30
miles away (unless it is to move to a different labor camp).
Zoos, museums, libraries, airports and art galleries are
unknown and unexplored.

14. The Mexican-American family is generally close knit and
usually requires its members to begin assuming responsibility at an early age. Tests conducted by the California
State Department of Education in Wasco, California, in

1968 showed that Mexican-American children scored "considerably higher than the middle-class normative population" in social ability and adjustment. Major examples of cultural values cited by the report as the cause of this finding were emphasis on (1) self-care of children at an early age, (2) care of younger siblings, (3) significant housework assignments, (4) helping to earn income and (5) sharing in adult decision-making. These skills will help the Mexican-American child to do well in school. However, these skills are not measured by IQ tests and are not reflected in the overall score.

15. Experiments have uniformly proven that IQ scores jump with change in cultural environment and family income. Studies show relative variances of 30-50 IQ points upon changed circumstances.

16. IQ tests presently used to assess school children relate in subject matter solely to the dominant culture and they were established solely by testing members of that culture. The Stanford-Binet test was standardized, i.e., its scales were constructed, in 1937 by giving the testing to 3,184 subjects. *Every* subject was a white, native-born American. The test has not been standardized since 1937. Even rural white America is clearly underrepresented in the sample group. The WISC test was constructed in 1950 by testing 2,200 subjects. Again, only Anglo-American children were tested and again there has been no re-standardization.

17. As a direct result of being placed in an EMR class, plaintiffs and the class they represent are being denied their right to receive an education, their right to equal educational opportunity and their right to not be placed in a segregated classroom, as guaranteed by Federal and State law and the Due Process and Equal Protection clauses of the Fourteenth Amendment of the Constitution of the United States.

18. Unless plaintiffs and the class of bilingual or Spanish-speaking children in EMR classes are taken out of the Educable Mentally Retarded program, placed in regular classes

and given intensive supplemental training in language skills and mathematics to allow them to catch up to their peers, they will continue to suffer the immediate and irreparable injury of a grossly inadequate education and the stigma of the label "mental retardation."

The next paragraphs in the Complaint set forth the statistics in Soledad and statewide. The facts of the meeting with Wendall Broom were also set forth, including the school district reneging on its promise to reassign. The complaint concluded by stating the irreparable injury the status quo was inflicting and requesting the relief outlined above.

# Chapter 28
## THE REQUEST FOR IMMEDIATE RELIEF

The *Californian*, the *San Francisco Chronicle* and the *Los Angeles Times* covered the filing of the *Diana* case. After the detailed complaint was filed, Marty and Mo applied for an immediate temporary restraining order, or TRO. It called for immediate cessation of the use of IQ tests in a language foreign to the test subjects and the removal of the nine Soledad children from the EMR class (or immediate retesting if the district could prove the Ramírez tests were unreliable). They began preparing for the hearing in San Jose on their request.

Mo was naturally concerned, especially because he was a relatively new lawyer. "What defense will the state offer in support of what they are doing to these children? How can we get ready to take them on?"

"As for testing children in a language they don't speak, there just is no answer to that imaginable," Marty responded. "They have no defense. The cultural bias of the tests will require a trial with experts, but it's hard for me to imagine the state attempting to justify the 13,000 more Mexican-American children in retarded classes, unless it wants to argue that Mexicans are just dumber."

"So you don't think," Mo asked, "that the state will endorse or attempt to use the eugenics publications of William Shockley at Stanford and Arthur Jenson at the University of California that attribute to white people a naturally higher intelligence than African Americans and Hispanics?"

Marty shook his head. "I have a hard time imagining California officials in the Department of Education taking such an extreme position. We'll see soon enough, though."

Marty was correct in his prediction of the State's position in the short run, but was wrong in the longer term. The state's position evolved later in the decade to one of embracing the notion that "retardation" occurred more often with minority children.

As required, CRLA notified the California Attorney General's office on the date that it filed the *Diana* case that CRLA would be asking for a TRO from Judge Peckham two days later, on January 9. Assistant Attorney General Asher Rubin, who would be the lead lawyer for the California Department of Education throughout the decade, appeared on that date for the defendants in the San Jose Federal Courthouse. Both sides filed opening papers with the court.

Marty and Mo met early in the morning on January 9 at the courthouse in San Jose. The two of them and Assistant Attorney General Asher Rubin waited anxiously in the courtroom while Judge Peckham reviewed the papers in his chambers. The preliminary position of the state in its opposition to the TRO was that it had been given very short notice, and no drastic change should be made, indeed no change at all should be made, at least until it had had some time to review the allegations and formulate its response.

After some time had passed, Judge Peckham came out to the bench and told the parties he had reviewed the filings, and that the allegations presented by the plaintiffs were very serious. He decided not to enter a TRO at that time, but he was not going to let much time go by before addressing the requests of the Soledad Children and the class they represented. He turned to Assistant Attorney General Rubin and asked, "Is the state truly giving IQ tests to children in a language they don't understand? How can that possibly be the right thing to be doing?" He then asked Rubin with visible impatience, "How much time do you really need to put together a response?"

Rubin answered, "I have already been instructed by Attorney General Thomas Lynch and by State Superintendent Max Rafferty to attempt to work with CRLA to achieve a rapid agreement on a substantial alteration of current practices. But, we need some time to see if that can be achieved."

Marty interjected, "Your honor, while our clients would like nothing better, attempts to work with the Soledad School District have failed, and it is imperative, at least for these children, that there be no delay."

Judge Peckham looked over sternly at Rubin and announced, "I am pleased to hear that the state is ready to work right away on making real changes. If what the plaintiffs have alleged is anywhere near accurate, you can be sure this court will be taking some action, if the state does not."

Judge Peckham then signed an Order to Show Cause as to why a broad preliminary injunction should not be issued against the school district and the state, scheduling a hearing on the matter two and a half weeks later, on January 26, a date that was later extended as intense negotiations were going in a positive direction.

# Chapter 29
# THE SUPERINTENDENT OF PUBLIC INSTRUCTION

Section 2 of Article 9 of the California Constitution provides for statewide election of a "non-partisan" Superintendent of Public Instruction. The superintendent implements policies set by the California State Board of Education on and for local school districts and directs California education. First elected as the twenty-second superintendent in California in 1962, Max Rafferty was finishing his second term in early 1970 and had made it clear he would be seeking a third. He was the antithesis of "non-partisan." Rafferty was born in 1917 in New Orleans and was raised in Sioux City, Iowa. The family moved to Los Angeles in 1931 and Rafferty attended Beverly Hills High School, UCLA as an undergraduate and then USC for his Ed. D. degree in 1955.

Rafferty was a right-wing firebrand as an undergrad, allegedly physically attacking the editor of the "radical" (his word) *Daily Bruin*. Rafferty initially worked as a classroom teacher for a Mojave Desert school system. After the conclusion of World War II, he held a variety of jobs as principal and superintendent in districts in southern California, including Big Bear, Needles and La Canada. As Superintendent of Public Instruction, Rafferty was an unabashed anti-progressive. He moved aggressively to control and censor books in the classroom, threatening to revoke the teaching credential of any teacher who used books he considered obscene, including *Soul on Ice* by Eldridge Cleaver. He advocated for the elimination of psychology courses from all curricula and attempted to ban

*The Dictionary of American Slang* from libraries at public schools. He railed against sex education and busing.

When Marty arrived in Salinas in early 1967, after taking the bar exam in Los Angeles, Bob Gnaizda advised, "We need to register as Republicans to confuse our local adversaries and use that affiliation to forge relationships with individuals who might otherwise view us as 'lefties.'"

Marty laughed. "So you think they'll look past my beard and mustache and longish hair to see a Republican?"

Superintendent Rafferty had entered the Republican primary to challenge the politically moderate incumbent Thomas Kuchel, a popular US senator. Voting in the primary for Kuchel seemed attractive, so Marty joined Bob on the rolls of registered Republicans in Monterey County. Rafferty's campaign pushed all of the ultra-conservative buttons, including such outlandish ideas as shooting a robber on the spot because "since we crawled out of the cave," retribution has been the only course of action that works.

In one of the biggest senatorial upsets in California history, Rafferty defeated Kuchel in the Republican primary. A relatively unknown candidate named Alan Cranston won the Democratic nomination. After Rafferty was nominated, Marty immediately re-registered as a Democrat (but Bob stayed the Republican course permanently). Cranston won by 350,000 votes (51%-46%), despite efforts by Rafferty supporters to paint Cranston as a communist. With the win, Cranston launched his highly distinguished career as a champion for progressive causes. Subsequently, Cranston was elected to the United States Senate three more times, served as senate whip for fourteen years and was a staunch advocate for and defender of the Legal Services Program in general and specifically CRLA. After Rafferty failed in his bid for a third term as superintendent, he left California to become a faculty member at Troy State University in Alabama. Later he joined the presidential campaign of Alabama governor and segregationist George Wallace. A more unlikely ally than Rafferty would have been hard for Marty and Mo to conceive of.

In the course of the CRLA's Education Task Force research, one of its members had found a helpful quote by Max Rafferty about testing, and Marty and Mo decided to set it out in the complaint for a bit of extra credibility and in the faint hope it would appeal to the superintendent. They stated, "State Superintendent of Public Instruction Max Rafferty has publicly gone on record stating that a child who can't be tested in his own language shouldn't be tested at all. 'If the test is discriminating against a kid because he speaks Spanish, then the test is wrong and should be discarded.'"

There was nothing shy, quiet or indecisive about Superintendent Rafferty. In early negotiations between Marty and Assistant Attorney General Asher Rubin, Rubin revealed that Rafferty was livid about what the schools were doing administering IQ testing in English to non-native speakers on his watch and without his knowledge. He apparently demanded that his attorneys and the Department of Education fix it and get it done overnight because it was just wrong. Early skepticism in negotiations thus gave way to intense, earnest and productive discussions and drafting sessions with CRLA, the California Attorney General and the California Department of Education staff working together in good faith at virtually break-neck speed.

# Chapter 30
# PROFESSIONAL PSYCHOLOGIST AFFIDAVITS

January 1970 was a month of limited sleep for Marty Glick and Mo Jourdane and the team helping them. Their work on the *Diana* case was going forward on at least three tracks: the negotiations with the State of California agencies, the completion of affidavits from the experts, Dr. Ramírez and Dr. Moreno, and the collection of sworn statements from parents and school officials from other school districts around the state. Marty and Mo and their colleagues collected, between January 10 and February 5, 1970, affidavits covering schools in Los Angeles, Napa, Butte, Glen, Yuba, Sutter, Modoc, Stanislaus, Santa Ana and Santa Cruz counties as well as individual districts in Modesto, Ukiah, Cutler-Orosi and Newell.

In addition to providing his test results and in-depth reports on each of the nine children in the Soledad EMR class, Dr. Ramírez in his affidavit reiterated the limitations in using IQ test scores, particularly with children from diverse cultures, to determine placement of those children in classes out of the mainstream. Importantly, he endorsed as an interim solution (until fairer tests were designed) the use of just the non-verbal section of the WISC IQ test as a floor for EMR placement of bilingual students (and those who primarily spoke any language other than English).

Steve Moreno, in his affidavit, explained his own extensive research and the findings he'd compiled in his article from May 1969 and his professional opinion that the appropriate steps to take included the use of the non-verbal section of the WISC in the interim as a barrier to EMR placement.

Over the Christmas holiday and the early weeks of January, CRLA amassed an overwhelming amount of evidence which was submitted to the court ultimately in the form of signed affidavits. The evidence proved that the Soledad practices were far from exceptional. In fact, the affidavits presented a damning picture of how local school districts, enabled by school psychologists who had failed to execute their professional duties properly, were ruining the lives of children.

Despite the fact that the parties had virtually reached an accord on the resolution of the lawsuit by early February, CRLA was determined that its new statewide evidence be made public and that Judge Peckham, who was to preside over the entire course of the litigation, see and appreciate it. Thus on February 5, 1970, CRLA filed all of the affidavits with the court. They told the following distressing stories:

Alan Arrow, the Assistant to the Head of Special Education for Los Angeles County, was interviewed on January 20 1970. He said that he did not know of any bilingual testers anywhere in that vast county and that bilingual families had no right to demand such testers anyway. Without a hint of embarrassment at the irony, he said that the only right these families had was to be told *in Spanish* of the school's decision on where their child was placed. He affirmed that while Spanish-surname students were about 19% of the county school population, they were more than 30% of the students in EMR classes in LA County.

CRLA attorney Gene Livingston in Modesto interviewed Dr. Harold Clark, a psychologist and director of the Stanislaus County EMR program. Clark affirmed that, although he was responsible for testing in nine of the fourteen county districts, he had employed no tester who spoke Spanish and, thus far, all tests there had been given in English. In response to direct questions posed by Livingston, Clark also candidly admitted that, "It would make no difference [testing in Spanish] because the tests are culturally biased against the Mexican-American students anyway."

The brothers Jesús and Pedro Partida provided affidavits about their experiences in the Napa Unified School District. They came from a Spanish-speaking home and were both transferred to EMR classes when they entered the second grade. Their mother had protested but proved powerless to prevent it. The brothers first believed that the classes were remedial in nature but soon learned that their curriculum was a succession of baby books, peg boards and puzzles. When they were in fourth grade, they were required to spend time, which they hated, with first graders, singing with them and playing toy flutes. Protests and requests for real textbooks were met with denials and discipline. Jesús was required to do work as a janitor's helper during school hours. Pedro did other work for the school and testified that he was promised $.25 per hour, which he was never paid. Pedro unloaded trucks, made wooden horses and "broomed out" and washed school buses and later sanded down metal bars in the buses. Both brothers were sent out, when they should have been in school, to assist in the harvest in Napa County and were paid $.40 per box picked. They wrapped Red Cross boxes to send to Vietnam during school hours. They were sent occasionally to do work at the local fairground. Pedro testified that a fellow EMR student had been assigned to help dig a ditch on the school grounds. All attempts to get in normal classes were rebuffed, even though both boys knew math and had taught themselves to read. They were sent to a succession of schools, always in EMR classes. Pedro related that in junior high, "The other kids [would taunt]: 'Look at the MRs, so we would sneak out a side door to avoid them.'"

Stephanie Rogers, a Vista volunteer working with CRLA, interviewed a variety of psychologists and officials in small counties and districts in Northern California. None had employed qualified testers who spoke Spanish, so they tested students in English. These officials confirmed that placement in EMR classes was based on the IQ tests, but some said they were working to "clean up the situation." One of the individuals Ms. Rogers interviewed, the Director of Social Services in the Chico Unified School District, was already aware of the CRLA lawsuit. He said that,

"The EMR classes are being slowly reduced in size as many children are found not to belong there."

A Modoc County parent, Ignacio Hernández Jiménez, filed an affidavit that he had three normal children all assigned to EMR classes based on IQ tests given "by a lady who only speaks English." He said, "Other children make fun of our children. Our kids do not like to be in the special class. Ignacio, Jr. tells us he wants to quit school soon. He is only thirteen years old." Attorney Joe Ortega testified about similar problems in Orange County and about a suit he had filed there to have kids placed in EMR classes retested.

Another declaration discussed EMR placement in the Cutler-Orosi School District, where the psychologist there had a unique system to cope with test bias. He simply added ten IQ points to the score of any child from a Spanish-speaking home. Unfortunately, that dispensation was mitigated by the fact that Cutler-Orosi subscribed to the view that a score of 80, instead of 70 or below, merited placement in an EMR class.

A Ukiah County parent related that his monolingual Spanish-speaking children were placed in an EMR class based on tests in English given by a non-Spanish speaking psychologist working in that district. Another parent with children in the Woodlake Union District testified to the same practice there.

Finally, CRLA attorneys Bob Johnstone and David Fielding provided their own and five other affidavits from parents in the Brawley and Calexico districts in Imperial County near the Mexican border. Dave Fielding met separately with two administrators working in the Calexico District. His affidavit recited:

> Both persons preferred to remain anonymous for fear of reprisal. Ultimately, both administrators admitted that a number of children were improperly assigned to the EMR classes. It was explained that in some instances they were placed in the EMR class merely because they had become *discipline* problems which the (classroom) teacher felt were too difficult to handle. . . . [Other] children were assigned to the EMR classes as the result of testing that was conducted by a doctor who was unable to communicate with the children in

their Spanish language and who administered standard English language tests without any attempt to translate or compensate in other ways for the child's language deficiency.

The two administrators also volunteered to Fielding their feelings about the bias of the tests: "An example of one question was a request that the child estimate the distance from New York to Chicago, difficult for children who likely had never heard of 'Chicago.'" Finally, the administrators told Fielding that a bilingual administrator had retested high school children in Calexico EMR at the beginning of the 1969 term, "corrected for cultural bias," and five children improperly placed had been removed as a result. But both said that there were still those in the Calexico district who had "misguided views of the limitations of IQ tests and purpose of EMR classes."

The Brawley testimonies from several parents—Elvira Galván, Jesús Noreiga, Angela Hogan, Genaro Carpio and Rosie Esquer—were no different. In each case, their Spanish-speaking children had been tested in English with no adjustment for the test's bias. In each case, a school nurse or principal told the parents of the results and that their children would be better off in a "special" class. None understood at the time that it was a class for the Educable Mentally Retarded. None was given an option to decline. The children were given one 45-minute period of real instruction a day but were not allowed to take their books home to study. The rest of their day was sewing, cooking, janitorial or schoolyard chores, singing and games.

Assistant Superintendent Donald Weber in Brawley frankly said that all testing was in English and "the results for a non-English speaking child will always be poor." He said it would be a "very valuable change to require that Spanish-speaking children be given tests in Spanish and that those administering the tests be capable of communicating with the children in their native language." Despite the numerous resources of Spanish-speakers in Imperial County who would have helped for little or no pay, this same superintendent had not availed himself of any translation assistance.

# Chapter 31
## NEGOTIATIONS WITH THE SOLEDAD DISTRICT AND THE STATE

With the *Diana* case on file, negative publicity for the Soledad school district had followed. Superintendent Bloom reached out to CRLA on Friday morning, January 9, two days after the filing. He reported that the district had agreed to implement immediately the original proposal discussed with the CRLA attorneys in mid-December 1969. He further promised to provide CRLA a copy of a written transition plan for each student.

As a result, on Monday, January 12, the district moved all nine children out of EMR classes and placed them in various regular classes, and the school submitted to CRLA the detailed written plan for daily classroom assignments for each child. The oldest student, Margarita, was transferred to a regular seventh-grade classroom to join students her age for social studies, math (with special help from the teacher and "classroom aides" as needed), home economics and physical education. The school provided her a "special development reading class of small group instruction" for 88 minutes per day, with a commitment to use other program funds to provide supplementary lessons as needed.

María was transferred to the sixth grade with regular classes in science, physical education, health, art and social studies. The school also provided her supplementary lessons in reading, language development, vocabulary, spelling and mathematics.

Arturo, Ramón and Rachel were each placed in separate fifth-grade homerooms, classes with 22-25 pupils that already worked with individualized programs. Similar plans were to be developed for all three in health, social studies, art and language skills. Special thirty-minute math assistance was scheduled for after school three days a week, and the school also provided them a special reading teacher for fifty minutes daily.

The Soledad school moved Manuel from EMR to the fourth grade. His program was identical in extra assistance and individualized planning to those of Ramón, Arturo and Rachel. Ernesto was placed in the third grade with the same resources and plans. For the twins, the school would first meet with their parents to discuss their absences, and they would likely join Ernesto in the third grade.

At least for some time, the parents of the plaintiff children reported that the district did provide the promised help. The district also agreed to permanently erase or seal all reference in the student's records of their IQ scores or the fact that they had been in EMR classes.

Meanwhile, the California Board of Education demonstrated its commitment to change by adopting on January 11—two days after the hearing on the proposed restraining order in San Jose—a resolution to repeal and replace key regulations that dealt with EMR classes, testing and placement. Assistant Attorney General Asher Rubin and Department of Education leaders negotiated the newly proposed regulations and the other terms of the settlement with Marty.

On January 16, Glick and Rubin signed a stipulation reciting their progress and asking Judge Peckham to postpone the Show-Cause hearing set for January 26 until a date in February, so the parties could continue to work on the settlement. Judge Peckham granted that request and reset the hearing for February 27.

By the end of January, an agreement in principle between CRLA for its clients and the state was achieved. Entirely new official California Department of Education regulations became effective on February 1, 1970. Marty Glick and Asher Rubin signed a comprehensive stipulation and settlement agreement on February 3. The terms of the settlement and class-action rules required that the stipulation be approved and made into an order of the court, and on February 5, 1970, Judge Peckham formally approved and signed his historic *Diana* order. Only 29 days had elapsed between the case filing and the revolution in treatment of the California-wide plaintiff class of schoolchildren, including the children in the Soledad school district.

# Chapter 32
## THE FEBRUARY 1970 COURT ORDER

The stipulation, Judge Peckham's order and the newly adopted regulations provided in combination the following:

1. Each child had to have an individual evaluation before assignment to an EMR class, including an approved individual intelligence test given in the primary language used in the home of the student. The test was to be administered by a qualified professional "competent in speaking and reading the language used by the minor in his speaking and cognitive activity." The use of a qualified interpreter working within the school system was authorized where needed. The new rules were not limited to Spanish-speakers but applied also to the substantial number of Chinese-speaking California school students as well as to any other primary language any individual student spoke at home. If a student scored above the two standard deviation IQ score cut-off on the non-verbal section of the IQ test alone, the school was prohibited from assigning that child to an EMR class.

2. Consideration of placement in an EMR class could no longer stop with an IQ test result. A local admissions committee was established to review, along with any test results, "a study of the cultural background, home environment and learning opportunities of the minor," as well as a report by a psychologist which was to contain any pertinent information in addition to just the test score. Use of a test score without consideration of the above factors was prohibited.

To make sure all these steps had been followed, the admissions committee was required to send a report of its actions to the district office, along with a certification that the parent or guardian of the particular child had been consulted. The new regulations authorized, if recommended, a "trial placement."

3. A new alternative called Integrated Programs of Instruction (IPI) was created and funded. It was available for children who were transitioning from an EMR class back to a regular classroom, as well as any other students for whom it might be appropriate. IPI placement required a local admission committee recommendation and determination that the minor could succeed in an IPI classroom. Placement included 120 minutes of instruction daily under the immediate supervision of the IPI instructor, instructional materials at the appropriate level and annual review with reconsideration as needed.

4. The California Department of Education agreed to mail to every school district a letter enclosing the new regulations, as well as several paragraphs that elaborated the changes being required. The opening paragraph of the required letter stated:

> It is the intent of the State Board of Education that all children who come from homes in which the primary spoken language is other than English shall be interviewed and examined, both in English and the primary language in his home. The examiner should take cognizance of the child's differential language facility. Any assessment of the child's intellectual functioning should be made on the basis of the spoken language most familiar to the child.

The letter called for retesting of EMR minors as described in the regulations with a report back to the Superintendent of Public Instruction. For students transitioning from EMR classes to regular classes, it required that they be moved to their new class level based on an individual assessment of the "developmental, social, physical and educational needs of the pupil" with a preference for placement with students of like age. The districts were also required to solicit input from persons most familiar with the needs of the pupil. For students transitioning from EMR to regular class, "supplementation should include as much individual, small group or other special attention as possible."

5. The Department of Education agreed to require each school district in the state to gather and report annually statistics sufficient to determine the numbers and percentages of the racial and ethnic groups represented in each EMR class in the district. Additionally, if there were a significant variance between any group's representation in EMR classes and their representation in the district, an explanation for the variance was to be submitted by the district. It was agreed that all reports received would be made available to Plaintiff's counsel for review.

6. The California Department of Education agreed to embark, and had embarked on, an effort to arrange a norming procedure for an individual intelligence test wherein the population will "be comprised of Mexican Americans who live in California." The state agreed it would make available the test developed to Plaintiff's attorneys and that, both before and after norming, it would provide the test on a confidential basis to Plaintiffs' experts credentialed by the California Board of Education. The parties agreed that upon successful completion and deployment of what they informally called the "Culture Fair IQ Test," including sufficient funding for the effort and publisher approval, the lawsuit would be concluded and dismissed.

The attorneys in the various CRLA offices and those in other legal services programs who had contributed affidavits were asked to follow up to make sure the changes were implemented in their communities. Indeed, in the communications Marty and Mo sent to their colleagues thanking them and asking for their continuing help, they wrote, "This case is an example of a successful court action which can become an actuality for our clients only if local citizens, community groups and concerned attorneys in California's 1,300 school districts aggressively seek compliance with the Court Order."

*Diana* round one was completed.

# Chapter 33
## DIANA PRESS COVERAGE

Judge Peckham's order became a national story overnight. The *Wall Street Journal* reported the story under a headline that read, "Court Orders Tests of IQ in Pupils' Home Languages" (February 6, 1970). The front page of the *San Francisco Chronicle* headlined "IQ Test Language Jinx Out" and recited the principal terms of the agreement; it quoted Mo and Marty as praising the cooperation extended by the California State Board of Education and the Attorney General. The *Los Angeles Times* writer Daryl Lembke filed an extensive story: "Schools Ordered to Revise IQ Test Programs: Judge Moves to Prevent Calling Children Retarded When Language Is Barrier" (7 February 1970). The *Los Angeles Daily Journal*, a publication established in 1888 and devoted to legal developments, carried the story on the front page on February 8, 1970. Wire services also reported the story nationally.

Sunday *San Francisco Examiner & Chronicle* writer Jim Wood covered the case in an expansive front-page story, reporting that the Department of Health, Education and Welfare officials in Washington intended to "follow the lead of the San Francisco ruling" on the national scale, stating that the decision "would be important not only to the Spanish-speaking, but to the Portuguese in New England and Chinese-speaking children as well." Wood included in his piece interviews with San Francisco supervisor Robert González and with Herman Gallegos, Executive Director of the Southwest Counsel of La Raza. Both cautioned that getting children out of EMR classes only to put them into the regular school system was not enough; it was imperative to fund and administer effective ESL (English as a Second Language) and bilingual education programs as soon as possible. That way, children who spoke another language could rapidly learn English while keeping up with their work in other subjects. Gallegos also pointed out that teacher and administrator attitudes that allowed children to be so egregiously misclassified in the first place needed to be corrected. He cited as an example a South Bay school district that exclusively put Anglo children in leadership positions over Mexican-American children. "When a protest was lodged," Gallegos reported, "the teacher explained that the Anglo children would be leading the Mexican-American children later anyway (when they grew up). The school, the teacher said, was 'merely preparing them for this role.'"

# Chapter 34
# THE LOMPOC DISTRICT PROTEST

The Lompoc Unified School District covers the town of Lompoc in Santa Barbara County and surrounding areas. It is the home of the Vandenberg Air Force Base. The Lompoc district was not happy with the plans for a new IQ test. In a letter sent to Judge Peckham on March 5, 1970, criticizing the stipulation and order, Irwin Wapner, the director of Pupil Personnel Services for the Lompoc district, asked if Mexican Americans would be the only ones for whom the test would be standardized and then used. Wapner asked if the state planned to have separate tests for the Chinese speakers of Mandarin and Cantonese and the many other distinct groups as well, and he noted the impracticality of such a process.

A test normed only on Mexican Americans was what the stipulation literally called for. Thus, Lompoc was not asking a bad question. While Marty and Mo were working on the stipulation, Mo had commented, "Marty, a test standardized only to Mexican Americans might never go forward when they start thinking about having tests for others, like Chinese Americans."

"You're right for sure, Mo. It does raise the specter of multiple tests for all sorts of cultures and languages. Once the state starts to work on it, I imagine we'll hear from them about that. But don't forget, Mexican Americans are by a substantial margin the largest minority group in California, and their percentage is increasing rapidly. So having a test addressed only to them is not unreasonable."

"What if the state comes back to us with this issue?"

"If they do," Marty answered, "we'll at least be able to insist that any new test instrument include a sufficient sample of Mexican Americans in the test base. Presumably, other minorities would be included as well to make it properly representative . . . before we'd agree to change the stipulation and ask Judge Peckham to change his order."

"And we'd have to demand the elimination of biased test items, such as the color of rubies, what is C.O.D.? and what is a chattel?" Mo added. "Good plan."

While the point made in the Lompoc letter about separate tests for every culture made sense, other elements in the Lompoc letter demonstrated why a court order compelling districts to make changes was essential. Apparently advocating for the continued inclusion of questions like "Who wrote Romeo and Juliet?" the director of Pupil Personnel Services for the Lompoc district wrote, "In a testing situation, where one is attempting to determine limits of *ability to learn*, there must be questions that children cannot answer correctly. . . . If the child has not had an environment that would help him to know and answer a question like this, this is an important factor to know as we attempt to determine *his top level of functioning.*"

All but the most biased of professionals would agree that the inability of a child living in a farm labor camp to answer a question about Shakespeare tells us nothing about that child's "ability to learn" nor his "top level of functioning." In this respect, the Lompoc letter spoke volumes about the depth and source of the problems created by reliance on the notion that intelligence is fixed and that IQ tests can identify those who cannot learn.

# Chapter 35
## CHANGES IN SOLEDAD

During 1970, Hector stayed in touch with the Soledad families to see how the transition was going. The families verified that all of the children were in regular classes and the threat of assignment of their younger ones to EMR classes was gone. The nine students were, at that time, getting individualized extra training in reading, language and arithmetic, and most said to Hector they were "doing okay." They reported that their classmates had stopped name-calling and that they were making new friends.

In March 1970, one month after the court order and about two months after the Soledad nine had been in regular classes, Mo, Hector and Marty visited Arturo at home in the labor camp and found him studying in the kitchen.

Mo asked, "So, *¿cómo estás, Arturo?*"

"*Estoy bien,*" he replied. "When I was in the retard class, the only math book they had there was second-grade. Now, I am already using a fifth-grade one and I can answer most of the questions," he said with pride. He continued with some enthusiasm talking about school and the changes and, on that day, his smile and joy made all the work on the case more than worthwhile.

Marty asked how the other children were doing.

"Some, like Manuel and Ramón, pretty good," he said. For others, like Armando, Diana and Rachel, he said, "It's still pretty tough."

As for Arturo, Marty and Mo wrote in an article in the March 1970 issue of *Noticiero*, the CRLA newsletter, "A month ago, Arturo's chances of finishing high school were slim. Now, it wouldn't surprise us to see him graduate from college."

# Chapter 36
## GETTING LEGISLATION PASSED

It was time for CRLA to take full advantage of its Sacramento office to cement and improve the changes set forth in the stipulation and Judge Peckham's order. As Mo returned to other pressing cases in the Salinas office, Marty went to work with CRLA Sacramento attorneys Jim Smith and Ed Kerry on new legislation.

In 1968, conservative Senator George Murphy had reacted negatively to the CRLA victories in preventing Governor Ronald Reagan from cutting Medicaid and the *bracero* litigation. At one point, Senator Murphy had introduced an amendment to the Office of Economic Opportunity (OEO) legislation that would have prohibited suits against any government agency by legal services programs on behalf of their clients, no matter how unlawful and harmful the act by the government was. That effort was defeated in the face of coordinated opposition by the American Bar Association, law professors, the national press and community groups. In 1969, Murphy introduced another measure that was defeated. The amendment would have prohibited the override of a gubernatorial veto of an OEO program in his or her state. That defeat became critical in 1970 when Governor Reagan did veto CRLA's 1971 grant, and an override battle ensued. Murphy was defeated in a re-election bid in November 1970 by CRLA supporter John Tunney. Richard Nixon won the Presidency in 1970 over Hubert Humphrey and John Mitchell became Attorney General. By 1970, the political landscape in the United States and in California was quite different from what it had been under the administrations of Lyndon Johnson and Pat Brown.

As the Sacramento office staff huddled with Marty to plan a legislative strategy, it was more apparent than ever that CRLA would need bipartisan support to navigate any bill through the legislature and have a chance at Governor Reagan signing it into law. It certainly could not be legislation openly influenced by CRLA.

A bit of research provided a possible answer. San Diego conservative Republican State Senator Sinclair "Clair" Burgener had been active in reforming special education, sponsoring legislation in 1963 that required classroom training for the intellectually impaired. Senator Burgener's own son Rod was developmentally handicapped. CRLA's Jim Smith spoke with the senator's staff; they indicated that Burgener would agree to a ten-minute meeting on the subject. Thus, in March 1970, Jim, Ed and Marty had their initial meeting with Senator Burgener and his staff; there would be many more in the following two years.

Burgener served on multiple committees and with several organizations that worked to secure the rights of the mentally handicapped. Although quite conservative, Burgener was known for crossing party lines to work with Democrats on issues that benefited his constituency or furthered his view of what was right. Early in his career, he refused a large contribution because he did not want to appear to be willing to have his vote bought.

At the meeting with Senator Burgener, Marty explained the facts of the *Diana* case and showed the senator some of the affidavits.

Just as Marty was gaining steam, the senator stopped him and said, "Hang on for a minute." The Senator called in an aide and instructed him to, "Postpone or cancel all my other appointments for the rest of this afternoon." The senator met protests from the aide with a look that communicated that the senator was not changing his mind.

Burgener listened and asked questions for at least an hour and a half. He was not only struck by the injustice to the Mexican-American children who were not mentally handicapped, but, as he observed, classrooms mixed with children who were in fact developmentally disabled and those who did not belong there meant that no one would have a program that fit his or her needs. He agreed to sponsor and campaign hard for reform legislation. Burgener was good as his word and subsequently worked to secure co-sponsors for relevant legislation. He argued eloquently in committee hearings and on the California assembly and senate floors for the bills that were drafted by his staff and CRLA attorneys, working together.

SB 1317, sponsored by Senator Burgener, was a bill to codify and expand the provisions in the stipulation, regulations and the court order. A companion bill was AB 2369, sponsored by Democratic Assemblyman Walter Karabian. One of Karabian's staff members at the time was Richard Alatorre, who had previously been involved in the EMR class issues as a member of the staff of the NAACP Legal Defense and Education Fund.

SB 1317 and AB 2369 were introduced as "urgency statutes necessary for the immediate preservation of the public peace, health or safety," and therefore they would become effective immediately upon passage "in order that pupils who have been incorrectly placed in classes for the mentally retarded . . . may be placed in a regular school program as quickly as possible."

Section 6902.06 in SB 1317 prohibited the admission of any child to a special education program for mentally retarded minors unless first tested with an individual intelligence test "in the primary home language in which the minor is most fluent and has the best speaking ability and capacity to understand." SB 1317 prohibited assignment of any child from a home in which the primary language was other than English who scored higher than two standard deviations below the norm on the non-verbal section of an approved IQ test.

Section 6908.08 in SB 1317 required retesting before the end of the 1970 calendar year of all special education second language minors according to the provisions of Section 6908.06 (This eliminated any notion in the court order that retesting was only an option.)

Section 6902.09 required parental involvement upon withdrawal from EMR of a minor who had been wrongly placed in the class and provided that the child would be placed in a compensatory education program or similar supplementary program "with the goal of accelerating his educational attainment so that he may participate in regular instruction of the district."

Section 6902.10 required annual reporting from the Superintendent of Public Instruction to the State Board of any substantial variances in racial or ethnic composition in special education classes and the general student population in any district.

Section 18102.11 and .12 provided for a two-year transition period and funding for the support of children removed from special classes based on retesting and a determination of improper placement. The mechanism selected for funding allowed districts to continue, for the two years, to receive the extra money that would have been allotted if the child were still in a special education class. These funds were specifically earmarked for supplemental assistance to transitioning students.

SB 1317 drew the all-out opposition of the California Association of School Psychologists and Psychiatrists (CASPP). On June 6, 1970, Dr. Rice of the Department of Education, speaking for the Department and CASPP, opposed the bill as too rigid and said that assignment should be left to the "unfettered" expertise of professionals. Marty provided background and testimony, and CRLA Salinas community worker Henry Cantú, who was quite articulate and obviously highly intelligent, was a very strong witness at the committee hearings as he told the legislators how he, himself, had been sent to EMR classes and kept there for two years.

During the senate hearing, Senator Donald Grunsky from Watsonville asked, "If school administrators are too stupid as to assign Spanish-speaking youngsters to EMR classes [who don't speak English], then what good would a change in the law do?"

Senator Burgener responded, "Don, the provisions in my bill will put a fence around that level of stupidity."

Orange County Senator John Schmitz, a member of the ultra-right-wing John Birch Society, asked if the bill needed amending to add that testing in the language of the child would only be "when practical."

When Senator Burgener responded that language like that would create a wide loophole, Schmitz did not push his amendment. Such was the influence and respect Senator Burgener had earned.

Eventually, the bill passed out of committee unanimously and was passed in the senate with little opposition. The real fight was in a key California Assembly committee hearing. After a hot testimony was provided on both sides, the members voted, and the bill prevailed by a single vote, 9 to 8, the majority needed.

In a second assembly committee, it passed again but only after an amendment that made the bill effective beginning in the 1971 school year (and no longer an urgency measure). With that, it prevailed on the assembly floor. The governor signed the reform legislation on September 20, 1970.

In 1971, Senator Burgener's follow-up bill, SB 33, requiring a complete psychological work up before a child was enrolled in EMR classes, also passed and became law.

In 1971, Assistant State Attorney General Rubin reported that the Education Department was working on the new IQ test and needed time for that process, an estimated two-to-three years. In the meantime, other concerns took center stage for CRLA, including the question of its own survival.

PART FOUR
# 1971–1972
# GOVERNOR REAGAN
# ATTACKS CRLA

# Chapter 37
# REAGAN ATTEMPTS TO KILL CRLA

CRLA has always spent more than three quarters of its time and resources helping individual clients with personal crises of one kind or another. In the year 1967, CRLA opened approximately 9,500 cases in its nine offices; the vast majority of them, about 9,100, were service cases. Service cases were individual client representations on matters personal to them: an eviction, a wage claim, an abusive spouse, a child custody dispute, an unemployment insurance appeal. The time sheets required of and kept by CRLA attorneys revealed that 80% of program time was devoted to service matters. In years that followed, CRLA's resources continued to be allocated in a similar fashion. These service cases filed on behalf of individual clients received little public attention, but were nonetheless important to each individual served.

By contrast, the CRLA impact cases received enormous attention. In 1970, some 1,300 separate articles appeared in some 150 different California newspapers about CRLA and its cases. Three quarters of the articles were favorable or neutral. Pressures from agribusiness and from state government agencies on the losing end of the CRLA's litigation to do something were mounting.

In July 1970, Governor Ronald Reagan appointed to head his federally funded California State Office of Economic Opportunity a deeply conservative CRLA-hater by the name of Lewis K. Uhler. Uhler had made a name for himself managing conservative John Birch Society member Congressman John Rousselot's campaign and then working with him in Washington, DC. Uhler's unabashed mission in 1970 was to abolish CRLA. He dispensed with the previously existing advisory committee to the state OEO because, as he tellingly intoned, "poor people should not make policy." He fired various professionals on his staff and replaced them with investigators he deployed to areas of California with CRLA offices; their mission was to gather evidence against CRLA to use in an anticipated veto of CRLA's grant by Reagan. To Uhler, the very notion that indigents should have lawyers to represent them against either the government or major corporations was unthinkable. *Newsweek* later quoted him, "Why should we pay the salaries of a lot of guys to run around and sue the state? The most a poor person is going to need a lawyer for is for some divorce problems, some garnishment problems. What we've created in CRLA is an economic leverage equal to that existing in large corporations. Clearly that should not be."

On December 1, 1970, CRLA passed its annual review with flying colors and was refunded by the OEO in Washington, DC, with a grant increase of about $205,000. Announcement of the refunding decision triggered the statutory thirty-day period during which the governor could exercise his veto power. In mid-December, Uhler began a campaign of selectively leaking to the press allegations of massive CRLA violations of both the law and its specific grant restrictions.

To prepare for battle, Marty called Bill McCabe of the prominent San Francisco law firm Jacobs, Sills and Coblenz. Bill had had worked with Marty in the Civil Rights Division and previously, with his wife Lucy Kelly McCabe, had run the Gilroy office of CRLA. By 1970, Lucy worked in the CRLA central office in San Francisco, where she provided litigation expertise to the field offices. Marty and Lucy asked Bill if his firm would provide pro bono representation to CRLA in connection with its refunding, if necessary. Bill accepted on behalf of the firm and said he would stand by.

On the day after Christmas, with four days left before the governor's right to veto expired, Reagan announced his rejection of the federal grant refunding CRLA based on a yet unpublished "Uhler Report." He stated that the 283-page report demonstrated multiple violations of the law and the conditions of CRLA's grant. He provided no specifics at that time.

On December 28, Marty, as the CRLA litigation director, wrote Uhler to request a copy of his report and the alleged 9,000 pages of underlying documentation. Uhler and his office did not comply, summarizing it to the media instead over the next two weeks. Uhler, however, did leak copies of his full report to prominent conservative publications, and their reporters ran highly adverse stories containing broad-based assertions that CRLA could only deny without specifics, having not seen the alleged basis for the accusations.

On January 7, 1971, a *Washington Post* reporter obtained a copy of the Uhler report and provided a copy to CRLA. It was a truly stunning document to read. The claims were so many and so substantive that the CRLA leadership were concerned that some of it might be true.

Marty asked, "Is it possible that any of this stuff could be going on in the program without us having a clue about it?" Director Cruz Reynoso responded, "It just can't be."

The most inflammatory charge was, "CRLA attorneys interceded [at the prison] in Soledad in an attempt to arrange a visit for the controversial American Communist Party leader Angela Davis to meet with imprisoned George Jackson, a prominent member of a Black Panther Party sub-group called the 'Soledad Brothers.'" This claim was sensational because activist Angela Davis had been accused of smuggling guns to Black Panthers to free their imprisoned members. The Uhler claim about CRLA and the prison in Soledad had no basis in fact whatsoever.

Other Uhler charges were a litany of claims that CRLA was a pawn of the United Farm Workers Union in violation of its grant conditions, handled prohibited criminal cases, engaged in massive ethical violations, deliberately brought frivolous suits and even went to court "barefoot."

Cruz Reynoso requested the leadership investigate all claims. Marty immediately convened a phone call with the directors of all ten offices to brief them on the report, and then he instructed them to leave no stone unturned in their investigation of each accusation. He asked them to report back accurately and completely: both the good and the bad. He gave them no longer than one week to find answers so that he and Lucy could produce for the OEO a thorough response to all of the accusations in the Uhler document. The order to the field offices included gathering affidavits to prove Uhler's charges wrong, as well as if any were accurate. It became immediately clear that nothing in Uhler's report was substantiated or true. Uhler had fabricated the Angela Davis claim. The report was a collection of uninvestigated and unsubstantiated complaints drawn from opponents, from out-of-context lines in newspaper stories and from unnamed sources. In almost all cases, the CRLA regional offices were able to demonstrate that the claims the report made were based on mistakes and lies.

In four days, Marty and Lucy McCabe had organized the responses from their regional offices into a point-by-point refutation, with sworn evidence obliterating each of the Uhler Report's allegations. Marty, Cruz and Mickey Bennett presented their "Memorandum of Fact and Law in Support of Immediate Refunding of California Rural Legal Assistance" to the OEO staff in Washington, DC, on January 13, only six days after they had first seen the Uhler manifesto; this was midway through the thirty days allocated for OEO to override the Reagan veto. Failure to override would be the death of the program.

Frank Carlucci was the acting director of the OEO at the time of the Reagan veto of the CRLA grant. It was later reported that he was experiencing significant pressure from Governor Reagan and his allies, including Attorney General John Mitchell. At the time there was speculation that Reagan might challenge President Nixon for the nomination in 1972. Carlucci announced on Saturday, January 30 at 7:45 p.m., that he was "sustaining the Reagan veto at this time." But, he also stated that he was simultaneously issuing a new six-month grant to CRLA while a thorough investigation of the charges would be undertaken. A copy of the Carlucci statement was hand-delivered to a shocked Mickey, Cruz and Marty at the OEO Washington, DC headquarters, where they were waiting, having been told by OEO staff members that an override was expected. OEO staff members also informed them that Governor Reagan would be making a statement shortly, and a television set was turned on in the room.

Reagan was addressing a meeting of some 800 delegates to the California Republican Central Committee in Sacramento, when he interrupted his prepared speech and said he had a very important announcement. With great drama and an ear-to-ear grin, he held up a sheet of typed paper and proclaimed that the Nixon administration had sustained his veto of CRLA's federal grant. The delegates simultaneously erupted in cheers and a standing ovation. It was stunning to watch. Marty immediately called Bill and Lucy McCabe to tell them they needed to galvanize the legal team. Bill agreed to meet with the CRLA leadership and immediately get up to speed on the case in order to guide the battle with Reagan and Uhler to a fair, public forum and away from the secret political sphere that had enabled private interests and conservative politicians to target CRLA.

# Chapter 38
# CRLA HEARINGS

In the following weeks, there was intense back and forth debate between Uhler and his collaborators, CRLA and its counsel and Carlucci and his staff as to the parameters of the investigation. When it became clear that Carlucci would appoint some sort of commission, the debate centered on who the commissioners would be, how they would be selected and how they would proceed. CRLA wanted public hearings; Uhler wanted them closed. CRLA wanted an adversary proceeding with witnesses and evidence and cross-examination. Uhler and his confederates wanted to submit their report and then hold secret, private meetings between the panel and the accusers, making the process political rather than truly fact-finding.

Decades later, it is hard to believe that the CRLA veto override by Governor Reagan and the proceeding that followed received extensive, continuous coverage in national and California publications. Sixty-nine California newspapers took editorial positions, with the substantial majority in favor of CRLA's request for an entirely independent commission rather than one appointed by the warring partisans; they favored an examination of the facts in a public forum. Prominent, nationally syndicated columnists, including Art Buchwald, Evans & Novak and Mary McGrory criticized Reagan, Uhler and the Nixon administration for dragging their feet. Both California senators weighed in repeatedly, as did scores of other politicians, bar associations, community groups and church leaders, all urging a public, evidentiary process.

A popular public television program at the time was the Peabody Award-winning series "The Advocates." Featuring USC law professors Howard Miller and William Rusher, it was set in a modified courtroom with arguments and witness presentations before a live studio audience. "The Advocates" decided to take on the CRLA refunding debate, and invited Cruz and Marty to attend and to brief the hosts Miller and Rusher before the show aired. Cruz and Marty ran into Uhler backstage; they courteously said hello and each extended their hands, but Uhler scowled and turned his back on them. The debate and audience response was animated and favored the idea of adversary-style public hearings.

In early February, McCabe successfully persuaded super litigators Jerome ("Jerry") Falk and Stuart Pollak of the firm of Howard, Prim, Smith, Rice, and Downs to join the CRLA legal team, and Bill introduced Jerry and Stu to Cruz, Marty, Lucy and Mickey, who reviewed for them the charges and counter-charges in the Uhler report. The CRLA team brought the two new advocates up-to-date on their debate with the OEO about the parameters of the investigation. Marty and Cruz had been insisting through OEO channels that separate funds be granted to CRLA to pay for the lawyers who would defend it in the proceedings to come.

On March 26, the Office of Economic Opportunity Commission on California Rural Legal Assistance, Inc. (OEO) announced the names of the commissioners, all distinguished and nationally respected judges, charged to investigate the Uhler charges against CRLA. The judges were Chairman Robert B. Williamson, a retired Chief Justice of the Maine Supreme Court; Robert B. Lee, Associate Justice of the Colorado Supreme Court; and Thomas Tongue, Associate Justice of the Oregon Supreme Court. All were Republicans, a fact welcomed by CRLA but not by Lewis K. Uhler. The OEO agreed to pay for CRLA's legal representation (but CRLA's lawyers subsequently had to file for an arbitration before they were paid).

Cruz, Marty, Mickey and their lawyers appeared for the first meeting with the judges scheduled for March 27, 1970, in Washington, DC. Despite the fact that clear written notice of the hearing had been given to both parties, no one showed up from Governor Reagan's office. The initial meeting was then rescheduled for

Wednesday, March 31, in San Francisco. Uhler attended this time, but proclaimed that neither he nor the State of California would participate in hearings that were public or adversary in nature. They would only cooperate, he avowed, if the commission was investigative, did not hold hearings except in private, engaged in secret *ex parte* interviews throughout the state and was willing to hear new charges that had not been included in Uhler's report (these new charges were to be delivered at an unspecified time). The commission members responded unambiguously. Chairman Williams said that the commission did not have investigative staff and would not be hiring any. "We will proceed like any court would, with evidence brought to us to be sifted by the time-honored judicial process."

Uhler responded that the judges were ill-advised or misled as to their role and refused to participate under those terms. With that, he walked out of the initial meeting. Behind the scenes, extensive lobbying by the Reagan forces was failing to change the format from public to secret and it became clear that the state would not be able to avoid having the evidence examined. Commissioner Tongue decided to resign from the commission when it became apparent that Uhler would not stand up to defend his claims and charges. On April 22, he was replaced by former Chief Justice of the Wisconsin Supreme Court George Currie, another Republican.

The commission began its business on April 26, 1970, in San Francisco and conducted fifteen days of hearings all over the state, including one non-public hearing at the Soledad prison. Uhler stayed in the background, but the commission allowed the many attorneys who were opposed to CRLA and the work it did to come forward with witnesses at all of the hearing locations, and they did so. Reagan called on the commissioners to resign, and Uhler made more accusations about CRLA instigating prison disruptions. Reagan later dismissively commented that the commission was only "fun and games" and that President Nixon would pay no attention to its findings.

The commission methodically heard all the witnesses and examined all the evidence offered, both in favor of and against

CRLA. Uhler's smear campaign did not distract the judges. On Friday June 25, the commission delivered its "Report of the Office of Economic Opportunity Commission on California Rural Legal Assistance, Inc. to the Honorable Frank Carlucci, Director." Immediately after receiving the findings, Carlucci reached out to CRLA and tried to negotiate a solution. He initially refused to give CRLA a copy of the report, and it was clear to CRLA's counsel from the tenor of the discussions that the report was very favorable. CRLA took a very hard line and refused to cooperate in any effort to quash publication of the commission's findings or agree to palliative new conditions on its grant, suggested by the OEO as a way to help Governor Reagan save face.

The New York Times did obtain a copy of the final report and, on June 29, informed the governor, the OEO and CRLA that the Times would publish its story about the outcome of the hearings and the commission's findings and reasoning that evening. Finally, just before the Times published the story, the OEO gave CRLA a copy of the report and a new, seventeen-month grant.

The "Report of the Office of Economic Opportunity . . . " cleared CRLA of all charges, said it was a model legal services program and that the work of the program was outstanding. The commission's conclusion was an unambiguous and complete vindication of the work of the program: "It should be emphasized that the complaints contained in the Uhler Report and the evidence adduced thereon do not, either taken separately or as a whole, furnish any justification whatsoever for any finding of improper activities by CRLA."

The justices, notwithstanding their Republican sympathies, did not hold back in condemning the Reagan administration, stating unanimously, "The Commission expressly finds that in many instances the California Evaluation has taken evidence out of context and misrepresented the facts to support the charges against CRLA. In so doing, the Uhler Report has unfairly and irresponsibly subjected many able, energetic, idealistic and dedicated CRLA attorneys to totally unjustified attacks upon their professional integrity and competence. From the testimony of the witnesses, the exhibits received in evidence and the Commission's examination of the documents submitted in support of the charges in the California Evaluation, the Commission finds that these charges were totally irresponsible and without foundation."

Rather than actually formally overriding the Reagan veto, Carlucci allowed Reagan space to withdraw the veto and, in a gesture to provide Reagan some cover, simultaneously granted new funds to the California state OEO for a so-called "Judicare" experiment.

Notwithstanding the crushing defeat handed to Uhler and the governor by the independent commission, Reagan declared victory, touting the decision by OEO to make the separate Judicare grant to his state OEO. He also alleged, without foundation, that the CRLA grant came with substantive new conditions, which had been negotiated by his team. The California and national press cited the commission's accolades for CRLA while laying bare the misleading and utterly discredited Uhler report.

CRLA had been consumed for seven months with its battle for survival, its staff was happy to get back to business, representing farmworkers and their other rural clients.

# Chapter 39
## *DIANA* SPAWNS THE *LARRY P.* CASE

In 1967, the OEO established the Reginald Heber Smith or "Reggie" program, named in honor of an esteemed legal-aid pioneer and former ABA President. First administered by the University of Pennsylvania and later by Howard University, the program recruited high-caliber law school graduates, trained them in poverty law and then placed them for a year or two in legal services programs around the country. In the eighteen years the program existed, it trained and placed approximately 2,000 Reggies. Several provided legal services in various CRLA offices.

In July 1970, Marty was approached by Mike Sorgen, a young Reggie working for the Mission office of the San Francisco Neighborhood Legal Assistance Foundation (SFNLAF). Mike, like many of the lawyers drawn to the legal services program in the early years of its existence, had achieved the kind of academic excellence that would have made him attractive to major law firms throughout the country. He had graduated *magna cum laude* with a B. A. from Brown and then received his law degree with honors from Harvard in 1967. He joined SFNLAF (pronounced *sniff-laff* by those who worked with and for it) after graduation from law school and his Reggie training. Mike had followed the *Diana* case closely. He had also done his own research on the very significant, continuing disparity between African Americans in the student population and their representation in EMR classes, particularly in San Francisco.

Mike asked if he and SFNLAF could serve as co-counsel with Marty on a class-action suit similar to *Diana*, but to represent the black students wrongfully placed in EMR classes because of culturally biased IQ tests.

"This lawsuit needs to happen, Marty," Mike pleaded, "but we're really busy at SFNLAF and resource-constrained with heavy workloads. It'd be much easier if CRLA, and you particularly, were willing to share your expertise and join with us in the effort."

"Absolutely," Marty answered. "CRLA serves many African American families and students in Seaside in Monterey County and in rural California. Attacking the IQ test bias to remove black students from EMR classes they were wrongly enrolled in is no less important than it was when our farmworker children were in the same situation. We're onboard."

In the following months, Marty and Mike met and brainstormed on several occasions, discussing how the *Diana* case would serve as a model for the intended case for black students. They concluded that, just as CRLA had engaged Chicano psychologists to retest the Soledad students and provide testimony, they should do the same as soon as feasible with prominent black psychologists willing to help.

That was when Bill Pierce came into the picture. Eradication of biased IQ testing of black children was number one on his list before he had ever heard of Marty, Mike, SFNLAF or CRLA. Dr. William (Bill) Pierce was a founding member of the California Association of Black Psychologists (CABP) in 1968. The CABP had already been actively lobbying for IQ test change.

At their first meeting, Dr. Pierce and Marty discovered they had both been involved in the civil rights movement in Ohio, where they had both attended The Ohio State University, as well as in the South. They exchanged knowledge about the history of IQ testing, and Dr. Pierce provided background on parent groups he had already been working with in the San Francisco School District. In particular, Pierce was working with the Westside Community Health Center, which had put him in contact with many parents and children in the San Francisco School District who might be willing to become complainants in the case they were building.

Pierce immediately brought onboard Drs. Harold Dent and Gerald West, two very progressive black psychologists willing to devote substantial free time to the issue. The first strategy meeting with all three of the psychologists focused on the question of retesting.

Dr. Dent said, "I get how effective it was for you, Marty, in your *Diana* case, to retest children who were first tested only in English when Spanish was their native language. I still can't believe districts did that."

"I totally believe it," Dr. Pierce said. "These districts just want minority students shunted aside so they don't have to deal with them by figuring out appropriate programs to address their individual needs."

Dr. West, who had been quiet at the beginning of the meeting, then spoke up. "Look, guys, even though our situation in San Francisco is different, what the *Diana* children and those in EMR classes in San Francisco clearly have in common is the underlying cultural bias against them in all of these so-called IQ tests. We need to work on stripping out those items that anyone should understand are biased. And we can retest from there."

Dent was circumspect: "I'm not sure about that, 'cause what we'd have if we just deleted test items wouldn't be standardized on anyone. But, at least with the three of us testing, we'll understand the lingo of inner city kids, speak with them about their background and be able to eliminate rejection of right answers that an Anglo tester may not get."

They agreed that, even if it would not be perfect, a retest could help convince a court that the children involved were not in fact "retarded," assuming that was their ultimate evaluation.

Pierce ventured, "Certainly our in-depth evaluation will be more credible than that of the SF District psychologists who never even talked to the students they purported to test."

The work of the three psychologists with community groups in San Francisco led them to parents in the district who were frustrated with the system and the way their children were wrongly placed in EMR classes. In 1971, a young boy named Larry P. and other children in the San Francisco district became part of that case. Dent, Pierce and West promptly retested them. In the course of their review, as planned, they used the WISC IQ test but noted and disregarded entirely a selection of highly culturally biased questions. The range of correct answers to the questions included culturally specific expressions and the retest was deemed by the psychologists to be more fair and accurate to the black children being assessed.

With positive results from the retest in hand, Marty was able to arrange a meeting for the Larry P. team at the Office of the State Superintendent of Public Instruction in Sacramento. Marty had made it clear that the delegation would be there to discuss the systematic discrimination in EMR placement of black students and that they would be seeking immediate redress.

They were greeted by state superintendent Wilson Riles, virtually unknown in politics before he scored a major upset by defeating his boss, the two-time incumbent Max Rafferty, to become superintendent. Riles was the first African American in the United States to be elected a state superintendent and the very first to be elected to any post in a California statewide election.

The CRLA and SNFLAF team found Riles to be engaging, but completely unwilling to act quickly or decisively in resolving the problem brought to him at the meeting. Riles recounted, "I have been telling parents for years, all your children need to do to get ahead is raise their hands and speak up when they are in kindergarten and first grade. That's what I did. Your teachers will think you're smart and pass that on to the next teacher, and then you'll have it made."

Riles had a negative reaction to suspending IQ testing and to retesting all black children in California EMR classes immediately, or to mandating any immediate change for that matter. He said that if black children were given special treatment or opportunities they might be seen as undeserving and unable to make it on their own. He said he was strongly opposed to "so-called affirmative action programs."

The CRLA and SFNLAF delegation was aghast. Riles' views and resistance were far from what they had expected. Riles concluded the meeting by saying he would continue to think about the issue and would look into it. CRLA and SFNLAF, nevertheless, were not going to hold their collective breath while they waited for Riles to act. They decided to focus instead on the district to see if bringing the matter to their attention might offer a better chance at affecting change.

In November 1971, the San Francisco Unified School District released a report that revealed that black students comprised more than half of all students in EMR classes in the district while representing only 25% of the school population. At the request of the Association of Black Psychologists, the district school board convened a special meeting to discuss the issue. Drs. Pierce and West and another CABP group member, Dr. Benjamin Criswell, made presentations to the board about problems and bias in IQ testing. The psychologists asked for an immediate halt to the testing. Dr. West emphasized that the use of IQ tests as they were then constituted was practicing "criminal negligence on the young mind."

Marty addressed the board to ask for an expedited further breakdown of the relevant district data. He pointed out that the discriminatory test practices used in San Francisco were very similar to those outlawed in the *Diana* case for Mexican-American children and that they had led to an extensive court order.

Martin Dean, Assistant Superintendent for the Special Educational Services Division of the district replied, "We cannot provide the data within the two weeks demanded by the association [CABP]." No further response was forthcoming from the district.

# Chapter 40
## *LARRY P.* IS FILED AND AN
## INJUNCTION ISSUED

When the *Larry P.* case was filed in late 1971, Mike and Marty lodged with the court a Related Case Memorandum that clearly associated the current case with the *Diana* stipulation and order, as the local court rules required. The "related case" policy of the district court was designed to allow the same judge to handle similar cases instead of having two different judges engaged separately and inefficiently in addressing the same legal issues. Thus, the Related Case Memorandum asked that the *Larry P.* case be assigned to Judge Peckham, because while *Diana* was dormant, it was still very much alive and on Judge Peckham's docket. Within days of its filing, *Larry P.* was assigned to Judge Peckham.

Wilson Riles and his team in the Department of Education in Sacramento were still not willing to agree to ban or limit the traditional IQ testing of black students. Therefore, the case proceeded. The first order of business was for plaintiffs to seek to "certify" the class. The lawsuit had been brought on behalf of all California black children in EMR classes, placed there on the basis of an IQ test. A class is certified, i.e. allowed, only if there are sufficient common questions of law and fact. Simultaneously with the class determination, Mike and Marty asked for a preliminary injunction against use of the IQ tests, the Stanford-Binet and the Wechsler.

On June 20, 1972, Judge Peckham issued his decisions, first finding that the class was a proper one and then issuing a preliminary injunction, prohibiting the defendant state and local officials from EMR class placement based on tests that did not "properly account for the cultural background of the students." His order was to remain in place until there could be a trial on the merits.

On behalf of the State Board of Education, Superintendent Riles promptly appealed Judge Peckham's two orders to the Court of Appeals for the Ninth Circuit. While the case was on appeal, further action in the district court was stayed. And the appeal was not decided until August 1974. Nevertheless, the fact that *Larry P.* was on file and assigned to Judge Peckham became important in 1973, when the *Diana* case roared back into action.

In 1972, Cruz Reynoso resigned from his directorship of CRLA to pursue other professional opportunities. The CRLA Board of Directors then appointed Marty to succeed Cruz and he became the third CRLA executive director in its history. Marty began serving in that role in June 1972 and continued as executive director until he joined the Stanford University Law faculty in the fall of 1974. Mo remained in the CRLA office in Salinas until 1975, when he left to work on the Jerry Brown campaign for governor. Both Marty and Mo remained in charge of all *Diana* case activities during their CRLA tenure.

# PART FIVE

# 1972–1979
# DIANA AND LARRY P. FIGHT
# TO THE FINISH

# Chapter 41
## BACK IN ACTION

From mid-1970 until the latter part of 1972, everything had remained relatively quiet on the California *Diana* front when it started a march back to center stage. Governmental entities stretching from Arizona to Massachusetts were seeking a plan to deal with similar problems in their states and had asked the California court for copies of its order and the agreement. But no further information had been submitted to the courts about the *Diana* litigation while the state was working on meeting its commitment, as outlined in the agreement: development of a replacement "culture fair" IQ test for Mexican Americans.

Federal judges will notice when matters languish on their official docket without an action plan. If nothing has happened in one of their cases for a substantial period of time, they send notices to counsel to ask for reasons why the case should not move forward or be dismissed. Judge Peckham sent out such a notice to the parties in *Diana* on September 8, 1972. The inquiry from the court naturally spurred CRLA and the California Attorney General to meet and discuss the progress in developing a new test and the compliance with the order by the school districts around the state. On October 31, 1972, CRLA and the Attorney General filed a joint submission with the court, stating that the Department of Education's "compliance (a new test) has nearly been accomplished" and that a meeting between representatives of the state, Plaintiffs' counsel, their consultants and a University of California-Berkeley professor working on a new IQ test was planned for mid-November. The filing also provided that the parties would report back to the court after that meeting, either with a joint agreement to dismiss the case as finished or with a request to set the case for trial. They promised to deliver their report to the court by December 31, 1972. The court accepted their joint filing and promise to report by the end of the year.

On December 8, the parties filed an updated status report stating they had met on November 20, as planned. The report pointed out that the state agreed it had not yet complied with the court order requirement to gather statistics for each district with an EMR program and, therefore, had also failed to ask those with a significant variance to submit an explanation. The state promised it would gather the statistics right away and send out letters asking for the explanations. In the conclusion of the report, the state discussed a proposed modification of the Weschler IQ test and affirmed that Plaintiffs' consultants would examine any such test. The next proposed meeting date for the parties was set for January 24, 1973, to determine where things stood. It all sounded positive.

# Chapter 42
## THE NEW IQ TEST

By the time of the January meeting in Sacramento to discuss the status of a new test, it had become apparent to Marty, Mo and their experts that the modified Weschler in its current state of development was not going to be a solution. The state indicated it had done some work with the highly regarded psychologist Jane Mercer; they said they had engaged her to develop a possible culture-fair test normed on the Mexican-American population, but no real progress had been achieved. Marty, Mo, Assistant Atttorney General Asher Rubin and Les Brinegar, Director of Special Education of the State Department of Education, all attended the January meeting, at which Brinegar informed Marty and Mo that the state was facing funding and other problems in developing a new and fair intelligence test. Brinegar asked them if CRLA had an alternate proposal that could settle their *Diana* case obligations.

By this time, discussions among members of the Association of Chicano Psychologists and other professional groups had given rise to serious questions about whether any new test, if labeled an IQ test and used as a measure of the child's capacity to learn, could ever be reliable for Spanish-speaking and culturally different children. As an example, Edward de Avila and Barbara Havassy wrote a paper that was later published by the Dissemination Center for Bilingual Bicultural Education entitled, "I. Q. Tests and Minority Children," in which the authors noted the problems of regional differences, even within the same language.

"Thus, while the word *tostón* refers to a half dollar for a Chicano child, for a Puerto Rican, it is a section of a fried banana."

They observed that Mexican-American speech is often different from standard, international Spanish. They cited differences in the "right answers" within Hispanic sub-cultures to questions on the Weschler, such as "What is the thing to do if you lose your friend's ball?" and "What is the thing to do if a fellow much smaller than yourself starts a fight?"

Another Weschler question they used as an example was, "In what kind of store do we buy sugar?" noting that for a particular Mexican-American child it might be "at the Chinitos," a colloquial term for a variety shop owned or staffed by an Asian family, while a different answer by another might nevertheless be correct (and both answers would be marked incorrect).

In any event, by early 1973, Marty and Mo and their advisory groups and community organizations were concerned about col-loquial reports of the number of children still in Educable Mental-ly Retarded (EMR) classes who did not belong there. This concern was compounded by the fact that the students might well remain there for many years while funding for a better test was not assured, and that this new "better" test might not work well any-way. CRLA, working with Senator Burgener, had locked into state law the IQ test barrier that prevented any Mexican-American or other second-language student from being assigned to an EMR class, unless he or she scored on the non-verbal section of an IQ test at least two standard deviations below the norm (and there was a required study of their adaptive behavior or out of school functioning and parent involvement and consent in the process).

Therefore, the invitation to offer an alternative solution to a new test was very attractive.

In January 1973, the State representatives met with Marty and Mo and, with some trepidation, provided them with the latest racial and ethnic statistics by school district. The CRLA lawyers were quite pleased to see that many school districts had eliminat-ed the overrepresentation of Latino children in EMR classes. How-ever, the percentage of Mexican-American children labeled men-tally retarded in approximately 235 school districts across the state remained unacceptably high. Mexican-American children represented 16 percent of the general student population while inching down from 26 to 24 percent of the students labeled Educable Mentally Retarded. That was still a very large disparity.

Some examples of district numbers that raised serious concerns included:

| DISTRICT | # MxAm in EMR | # Should Be |
|----------|---------------|-------------|
| Fresno Unified | 137 | 78 |
| Garden Grove | 166 | 57 |
| San Jose | 74 | 29 |
| Oxnard | 79 | 32 |

On February 7, 1973, Judge Peckham sent out a notice for a preliminary pre-trial conference for March 6. Then, the March 6 session was continued until April 16, when the parties jointly reported that they were making good progress. The state had finally requested, received and provided to CRLA in March the required explanations from each district. One district, the Fillmore Unified School District, reported that it had adopted a three-year "affirmative-action style" plan to eliminate its persistent overrepresentation of Mexican-American children in EMR classes. Their approach was modeled on plans that employers were using to make their workforces more diverse while still hiring fully qualified candidates.

Marty thought the Fillmore plan might be a perfect way to come up with the alternative to the culture-fair test requested by the Department of Education. He thought it had a very good chance of being acceptable because a school district and not CRLA had originated it. Mo agreed that this could very well be the way to go.

At the next meeting of the working group, Marty presented the Fillmore plan and suggested that it might be acceptable as an alternative to the development of the test normed only on and for Mexican Americans that the 1970 court order had mandated. The trade-off, he said, would be that the Fillmore school district's timetable and goals would be mandated for the approximately 235 districts that had a continuing statistically significant overrepresentation of Mexican Americans labeled mentally retarded and the plan for the new test would be dropped. Marty stressed that the Fillmore plan was not a quota system that mandated precise mathematical compliance. Instead the numbers were expressed specifically as goals, leaving districts free to explain any variances that might occur. The group agreed and asked Marty to put the suggestion in writing so the Department of Education could consider it.

On April 3, 1973, Marty wrote that CRLA had reviewed the racial and ethnic statistics and explanations furnished by the Department of Education which revealed the following.

(1) There is still an unacceptably large variation between the percentage of Mexican Americans in EMR classes and the percentage of Mexican Americans in the general school population (23.9%-16 %).

(2) This variance is not characteristic of most school districts but is the result of very large disparities in about 235 of the school districts in California.

(3) The most striking example of success in eliminating the variation is Los Angeles Unified, where there are 143,710 Mexican-American students (22.6%) in the general school population and 1604 (21.8%) in the EMR population.

(4) The real problem is reaching the remaining school districts and overcoming their inaction or recalcitrance so that the disparity can and will be eliminated.

Marty added, "The approach suggested by the Fillmore Unified School District is the one we might implement statewide. In the Fillmore District, Mexican Americans make up 44.1% of the student population, but are 61.8% of the EMR population. On December 18, 1972, the district submitted to the Department of Education its "Explanation for Variance." In that report, the district concluded: All personnel in the district realize that these explanations are not adequate to justify the discrepancy in percentages that do exist. In order to correct this situation, the following objectives have been set by the district personnel:

The percentage of Mexican-American pupils in the Educable Mentally Retarded classes in the Fillmore Unified School District shall not exceed these percentages by the dates specified:

DATE          PERCENTAGE
June 15, 1973  59
June 15, 1974  50
June 15, 1975  (equal to or less than the % of Mexican-American children in the total school population)

On behalf of the *Diana* Class, Marty's letter then requested a stipulated order be entered calling for the Department of Education to correspond with the problem districts to advise them of the success of most districts in the state and of the Fillmore plan. The state would mandate these districts to adopt a similar plan to eliminate present disparities. Districts would have to report yearly on plans and progress or face sanctions. Adoption of this order and compliance with it would close this case. The requirements in the order calling for the development of a new test instrument would be eliminated.

# Chapter 43
## THE NEW STIPULATION AND COURT ORDER

The CRLA and state lawyers, after much discussion, drafted their final agreement, which was, in all material respects, consistent with the draft Marty had sent to the state earlier.

On June 18, 1973, Marty and Department of Education representative Asher Rubin signed the new stipulation on behalf of the class and on behalf of the various state officials and submitted it to Judge Peckham at a hearing in his San Jose courtroom.

The Stipulation (and Judge Peckham's court order that adopted it) recited that:

(1) Most districts had eliminated the disparity (with examples given).

(2) A significant variance continued to exist between the number of Mexican Americans in classes for the Educable Mentally Retarded and their number in the districts at large in approximately 235 of the state's school districts.

(3) The court and the Department of Education had the authority to fashion appropriate relief to remedy past discrimination.

(4) A plan with goals and timetables must be adopted by each district with a statistically significant disparity and a three-year effort to eliminate the disparity would commence in September, 1973.

(5) The plan must include a program for special assistance in accordance with the individual needs of those students

removed from EMR classes as part of the effort to eliminate the disparity.

(6) If there was still a significant variance after three years, the state would conduct a "thorough audit" by persons other than district employees and with a "professional person representing the Mexican-American community as a member of the audit team." The audit would include reevaluation of students, if necessary.

(7) The previous requirement for a new test was eliminated.

The stipulation and order also provided that if, after five years, the affirmative action approach had been unsuccessful, the parties could seek further relief from the court, including cutting-off state funds for non-compliant districts. However, if success were achieved, the *Diana* case would be ended and dismissed. The parties agreed to a later insertion of the technical definition of significant variance in the stipulation and order because the parties did not want any further delay while that statistical formula was being technically defined.

Judge Peckham congratulated the parties for achieving this creative action plan together, and on June 18, 1973, he adopted the stipulation and formally entered it as his court order superseding the February 1970 order.

In March 1973, Marty and Mo had enlisted a probono statistician to double-check the accuracy of the calculations the state had previously provided to them. And, reasonably well-versed themselves at math and statistics, Marty and Mo had reviewed the calculations, understood that the ultimate standard for a significant variance would be one standard deviation and that, using that standard, the districts in which Spanish-surnamed children were over-represented in EMR classers would add up to the approximate 235 number. The state never objected to or contradicted the CRLA statements that the number yielded as significant by statistical analysis was approximately 235 districts. Months later, the state would pivot 180 degrees and argue that the 235 districts number was an "albatross."

# Chapter 44
## NEGOTIATIONS TO FILL IN THE BLANK

On June 26, when Mo returned to California from a three-month leave, he was elated to find a copy of the signed stipulation and court order on his desk. He called Marty.

"Hey, chief, I'm back. The state signed our order. Way to go! Really cool. Now what?"

"Thanks, Mo. It all worked out as we had hoped. Now that we have a new court order, we can really go after individual districts that have been resistant. And the state should be onboard to help us. But before we do anything else, you'd better look into the proper way to define 'significant variance.' We need to nail that down in proper language and ask the judge to insert it into the court order. Do you have time to talk with some experts to figure it out and then work with the state to finish out that part?"

"Absolutely. I have a list of some university guys I talked to. I'll get this done right away."

Mo spoke with a couple of statisticians at Stanford University and at the University of California Riverside to understand the specific formula for a significant variance between the percent of Latinos in the general population of each district and the percent consigned to the EMR class. Both statisticians agreed upon the industry standard square-root formula to define a significant variance at one standard deviation and indicated that it would be sound as a matter of statistics for both large and small districts. The formula was stated as the square root of II (100-II)/N wherein II is the percentage of Mexican-American children attending school in the district and N is the total number of children in the

EMR class. After applying the formula to the then-current statistics from the school districts, the result was that 238 of them had a significant variance.

Mo went over what he had learned from the statisticians with Marty. "You know, it turns out that forty-seven districts can come within the allowed variance by removing just one child from EMR. Should we just leave them out?"

Marty and Mo decided that exempting those districts was a gesture of fairness and goodwill. It would avoid for those districts the substantial requirements in the court order. Instead, they would concentrate on districts with a pervasive problem.

With that resolved, Mo contacted Allan Simmons, Chief of the Bureau of Mentally Exceptional Children in the Department of Education's Sacramento office to talk through the proposed articulation of the formula.

Simmons said, "You know, Mo, while the result seems accurate, I have some concern that your square root formula might be too complicated for districts to understand easily. Will you be satisfied if I can come up with the same thing but in the form of a chart or graph instead?"

"No problem, Alan," Mo responded, "so long as the results are basically the same. We don't care how the formula is expressed and we like making it easier to use."

"Okay, great. I'll go to work on this and get back to you with hopefully a practical way to express the formula, after I've reviewed it with my colleagues."

Mo left satisfied that the insertion of the formula in the order and in letters to districts would be resolved as a formality and without an issue.

# Chapter 45
# THE STATE TRIES TO EVADE THE COURT ORDER

The June 1973 stipulation and order had apparently produced a firestorm of protest from some affected school districts, but the two CRLA attorneys were never made aware of that fact. In addition to conceptual objections, the districts apparently had asserted that they lacked the funds to pay for the required transitional instruction (and did not want to reallocate the funds they had).

Equally unhappy was Superintendent Riles, who did not support anything labeled affirmative action; he had said as much in the 1971 *Larry P.* meeting. Riles had learned about the court order and stipulation after the meeting on the significant variance between Mo Jourdane and Allan Simmons and had become deeply opposed to it. When *Larry P.* counsel Armando Menocal wrote the Department of Education demanding that his clients be provided the same relief in school districts where African American children were overrepresented in EMR classes, fuel was added to the fire. Soon after the initial Simmons-Jourdane meeting, the Department of Education leadership instructed the Attorney General's office and Simmons to find ways to avoid or at least reduce dramatically the effect of the stipulation and court order.

On July 26, 1973, Allan Simmons wrote, responding to the proposed definition of significant variance with a wholly new proposal; no action would be required in any small school districts unless the number of Mexican-American students labeled mentally retarded exceeded the expected number of Mexican-American representation in the district by more than 10 students. Simmons proposal meant that, as a matter of basic math, no small district such as Soledad would ever have to make any change. Using the Soledad school district as an example, Mexican-American students constituted in 1970 about 35% of the general student body. Simmons' proposed formula would start with that; therefore, in a class of 12, the expected and proportionate number of Mexican Americans in the class would be 4.2 (35%). Simmons would then arbitrarily add 10 to the 4.2 to create the threshold for required action. Of course 4.2 +10 = 14.2 which was more than the total Soledad EMR class size.

The state proposal for larger districts added an extra 2% to the standard deviation and also added ten more students over and above the expected representation in EMR classes. This would have exempted most of these districts from the mandate to take any action. Under the department's new formula, the approximately 235 districts mandated to take action in the stipulation, the court order and all of the correspondence between the parties would be reduced to only 58. These 58 districts were only the truly egregious examples, and the rest would not be required to do anything at all to affirmatively address the inequities.

On August 15, 1973, Mo Jourdane and Alan Simmons met in an attempt to bridge the widening gap in the positions of the state and the plaintiff class to no avail. The next day, Mo wrote to Simmons a detailed letter reminding him (and the Department of Education) of their existing duties under the order. He received no response.

Assistant Attorney General Rubin had worked collaboratively with the CRLA attorneys in the past, expressing concern for the misplaced students. Thus, a direct call to him seemed appropriate. Marty called on August 28, and it became even more apparent that the state was backing away from its stipulation and from their obligations under the order. Two days later, on August 30, Mo and Marty traveled to Sacramento and met with representatives of the Department of Education and the Attorney General's office. Rubin opened the meeting by communicating that the Department of Education was no longer willing to consider any definition for or use of the significant variance. He further stated that the goals and timetables approach agreed to in writing just a little over two months earlier and embodied in an order signed by a federal judge was no longer viable, and there was no reason to discuss that any further. He offered up an assertion that the department could no longer follow that path because of a state statute, Education Code 6902.095, which required an explanation in the event of a 15% variance or higher in any district. Assistant Attorney General Rubin asserted that Code 6902.095 left the state powerless to do anything, unless the variance in a particular district was at or exceeded that 15% level. In other words, he was arguing that the statute legitimized no action by the state, except when the disparity rose to that level.

Education Code 6902.095 had been existing law when the stipulation was signed in June, but according to the state representatives, none of them had paid attention to it back then. In an affidavit later signed by Marty, he swore that the code section had been explicitly discussed during the meetings that led up to the stipulation and consent order, and no one had suggested then that it was any kind of obstacle.

Rubin also suggested at the meeting that it would be best to just wait for the state to adopt its long-overdue Education Master Plan to deal with the matter in a progressive and sensible way. In the meantime, the state would urge the districts where Mexican Americans were significantly overrepresented in EMR classes to "continue to work on the problem."

In an affidavit Assistant Attorney General Rubin filed when the case went back to litigation, he asserted, "When Mr. Glick and Mr. Jourdane . . . had recently discovered that their hands were tied by the 15% statute, they became enraged and made intemperate accusatory statements against me and the department. They stormed out of the meeting without giving the department a chance to explain its difficulty with the significant variance. . . . My next contact with them was when they courteously served me with the *Application Re Contempt.*"

What Rubin's affidavit didn't say was that three and one-half years had passed since the original *Diana* order was signed and still over 200 districts had too many Spanish-speaking students in EMR classes. What was not included in the affidavit submitted by the state was that the lives of the children improperly assigned were essentially being destroyed while they were held in those dead-end classes waiting for the districts to be persuaded to change their policies or for a Master Plan. And perhaps most important, what the affidavit did not reveal was the most startling statement made by one of the state officials at the August 30 meeting: "There are more mentally retarded children in black and Chicano ghettos, barrios and other poor neighborhoods than there are in communities like Beverly Hills, and so we should expect therefore to find more blacks and Chicanos in EMR classes, and for that reason the [previously agreed] formula will not work."

The affidavits later filed by Marty and Mo stated, "After defendants had finished stating their position, plaintiffs' attorneys specifically asked if the department had any proposals to offer for the definition of significant variance and offered to leave the room temporarily, if department officials wished to talk it over privately. After being informed that the department felt that there was no purpose in further discussion on that point, plaintiffs' attorneys quietly and politely left the defendants' attorneys' offices and returned to their own offices."

There was no doubt that the defendants had observed the anger and disappointment Marty and Mo felt as a result of the 180 degree turn, the stonewalling and the eugenics-reborn characterization that "more Chicanos and blacks than whites are retarded." There was no way the two CRLA attorneys would remain in the meeting after the state had declared its intention to repudiate the agreement and court order they had consented to just two months and twelve days earlier.

# Chapter 46
## THE CONTEMPT ACTION IS FILED

CRLA promptly filed papers to hold the California Board of Education and State Superintendent Riles in contempt of court and subject to sanctions for deliberately disobeying the order of the District Court.

The law provides two very different contempt of court remedies for violation of a court order. Criminal contempt can be sought for deliberate, willful and knowing refusal to follow an order. The less severe remedy of civil contempt, in contrast, is filed when the parties are essentially in disagreement about what a court order requires and one party is refusing to act in a way the other says is covered by the order. CRLA sought a civil contempt.

On September 6, 1973, the *Diana* class asked Judge Peckham for an order to show cause and set a hearing date for contempt proceedings. Attached to that request were affidavits from Marty and Mo setting out in detail the meetings and other efforts to make the state comply and the state's refusal to do so. The request for the show-cause order stated, "On August 30, 1973, defendants informed plaintiffs that they no longer agreed with the basic premises of the June 18 order and they would not send out letters to districts or make the identification of districts with significant variance or do any act to comply with this Court's order."

Judge Peckham signed an order to show cause on that day and set September 17 for a hearing on the contempt request. Thus, some three years and nine months after the filing of *Diana*, the bell rang for the first round of contested litigation, and it was no-holds-barred.

In response, the State of California filed motions and briefs to oppose the contempt order, arguing the following:

1. The June 1973 stipulation of the parties and the court order were void and unenforceable because they contained no mathematical definition of "significant variance." In response to the point made by plaintiffs that indeed approximately 235 districts was the number that resulted from a straight-forward use of one standard deviation (it was actually 238), Assistant Superintendent Rubin called the 235 number "an albatross" being "hung around [the State's] neck" and that the state had "never paid any attention to it" and "the court should not be mesmerized by it."

   The state claimed in their papers that only 56 school districts should be the proper number to include in mailings to districts, even if such mailings were to be required at all. The state even argued that "significant variance" was never meant to refer to any statistical concept or any formula. It was just a completely undefined (and undefinable) use of the word "significant" as a synonym for "meaningful," and the word "variance" only referred to an undefined "difference."

2. The *Diana* case should be consolidated with the *Larry P.* case into one action in the apparent hope that such a combination would create complexities and conflicts that might cause Judge Peckham to reconsider or narrowly construe his June 1973 order.

3. The case should be dismissed for failure to join indispensable parties, all 238 of the California school districts with what plaintiffs said was a significant variance. Thus, defendants Riles and the Board of Education were actually arguing for the first time, three and a half years into the case and after two settlements and court orders, that the case could not go on because the individual districts had not been joined as parties. The state contended that the superintendent and the state board were actually "powerless" to call dissenting districts into account. And rather than simply moving to add the districts to the litigation, the state asked

the court to terminate the case altogether because the districts were not parties.

4. Marty and Mo had acted unprofessionally and should be admonished by the judge for "shabby practices unworthy of the profession." One of the state's briefs stated, "Plaintiffs have sought to express their *pique* at the parties' inability to agree by citing the State Department of Education for contempt. This maneuver is puerile, and this court should not countenance the reckless use of extreme measures when the facts plainly indicate that the party to be cited has acted in good faith."

5. The presence in the law of a requirement for reporting when variances exceed 15% sanctioned and preempted any remedy for violations at other lower levels of unlawful discrimination.

6. The Superintendent of Public Instruction and the Board of Education (and the financial officer defendants) lacked authority to require action from the individual school districts. Thus, they claimed the state lacked the authority for the original order and stipulation in 1970 that required retesting, setting new standards, requiring interim supplemental instruction and compelling reports from the districts. And the submission of the mid-1973 stipulation to the court was a regrettable mistake because the state could not really do any of what it said it would do: send letters to significant variance districts, require a plan with goals and timetables for reversal of misallocations of Mexican-American children to Educable Mentally Retarded classes, investigate persistent problem districts, issue progress reports and ultimately agree that the court could consider requiring the department to withhold funds if it made the requisite findings of fact.

7. The existing court order might have the effect of preventing truly Educable Mentally Retarded Mexican-American children from getting into an EMR class.

As icing on the cake, the state made two further arguments that defined credibility:

8. The reduction of the number and percentage of Mexican-American students in EMR classes would have the inevitable effect of increasing the percentage of African Americans left behind in those classes, and that result (magnifying that separate injustice) should be avoided.
9. A family with "a great many retarded children" might move into a new school district and thus increase its numbers in EMR classes. Never mind that such an event would defy all odds and that the District would be free to explain this remarkable development.

What had begun as just one motion, the plaintiffs' motion for a finding of civil contempt and an order for the state to comply fully with the existing order, using the one standard deviation formula, had expanded to three separate motions. The initial date for the hearing on the contempt motion was set for September 17 but was postponed to October 11 to allow additional briefing on the state motions to dismiss and to consolidate.

CRLA attorney Fred H. Altshuler, who was working in the central office in San Francisco when the motions in *Diana* were filed, joined the team and took on as his primary responsibility the response to the lack of capacity argument and the cross motions filed by the state. Fred authored a concise and powerful response, citing both United States Supreme Court authority and several key cases from the United States Appellate Courts to the effect that a stipulation to a consent court order waived forever any claim that other parties had to be added or that the consenting party lacked authority to carry out the order.

On April 19, three days before the final hearing in the *Diana* case on the three motions, the state submitted an updated "Ethnic Survey of EMR Classes" to the court. The update did show a reduction of the number of districts with a one standard deviation or more disparity between Mexican-American students in EMR classes and in the general population of those districts, a welcome development that CRLA credited to pressure applied in those districts by community-based organizations. The submission by the state was not; however, just the new enrollment numbers for EMR classes from each district. The state, without seeking permission from the court to do so, also filed a short cover memo, which contained a new contention: "The expected incidence of mental retardation in the United States is 2%. It has been estimated to actually be as high as 7% in low socio-economic conditions where the prevalence of delayed or impaired development may be reflected in mental retardation." The state was suggesting that African American and Mexican-American children actually had more than three times the incidence of mental retardation than their mostly Anglo peers from affluent society. Indeed, the state even argued in this last-minute memorandum that "California may be under-enrolling [minority] pupils who need special learning help." In support of this contention, the state lifted out-of-context statistics from a then-recently released report authored by The President's Commission on Mental Retardation in 1974. Ironically, that report, relying directly on Dr. Jane Mercer, the very expert the State had hired to create a new IQ test, actually said the opposite. Dr. Mercer, in 1973, in her groundbreaking research quoted at length in both the *Diana case* and in the *Larry P. case,* had coined the terms "the Six-hour Retarded" and "Adaptive Behavior" in explaining the critical need to examine how the child performed at home and in his or her home environment before concluding the child was in some way mentally impaired. Specifically, as noted in the report the State was relying on, Dr. Mercer had studied Berkeley Unified School District Mexican-American students, 14.9% of whom had been classified by that District as "borderline EMR." Using her Adaptive Behavior Scales, measuring how those children performed away from home, she concluded in the very Report cited by the State that the real rate was just 1.53%.

With this tactic, the State in *Diana* (and to an even greater degree later in *Larry P.*) was endorsing the thinking of the eugenicists who had historically claimed that the very high and disproportionate IQ test diagnoses of retardation in Black and Mexican-

American populations was proof that their inferior ability was fixed at birth and natural.

At the hearing, Marty and Mo pointed out the flaws in the state's assertion that the Report suggested a greater incidence of retardation among Mexican-American and African American children. It actually contained many warnings about misclassification of Hispanics and African Americans and described in some detail a Milwaukee study that showed that minority children who had the assistance of enriching programs kept pace in their IQ scores with their Anglo peers.

The full hearing on the merits was finally held in San Jose on April 22, 1974. It went on for the better part of an hour with Judge Peckham asking hard questions and indicating his skepticism about the state's contentions. Rubin asked for further delays as the so-called Master Plan continued its development. Marty argued that the children wrongly placed in EMR classes could not and should not be forced to suffer an inadequate education any longer and that the state had no right to attack an order they had endorsed and stipulated to. Mo pointed out again that the one standard deviation formula fit the blank in the order like a glove.

The judge took the matter under submission and one month later, on May 22, 1974, he issued his stringent new order finding Riles and the other defendants in contempt of court. At the outset, he stated, "Claiming that the parties were unable to agree on a satisfactory definition of 'significant variance,' defendants subsequently refused to send out the required letters. Paragraph 3(a) of the stipulation . . . states that 'only in approximately 235 [of the districts in the state]' is the variance significant. It is quite clear from the stipulation itself, that on the basis of the data available in June 1973, roughly 235 districts were regarded by the parties as exhibiting 'significant variance.' It is likewise clear that agreement on a formula to express 'significant variance' was intended to require no more than the mechanical act of locating and designating an accepted statistical formula which would result in the identification of roughly 235 districts. One such formula suggested by plaintiffs is the recognized formula for calculation of one standard deviation from the mean of a given sample. Apparently, application of that formula to the data available in June 1973 would result in the identification of some 238 districts exhibiting a significant variance.

"Defendants, in contrast, have suggested various formulae and criteria which would single out approximately 50 districts. Such a drastic reduction in the number of districts can be construed only as an attempt to curtail severely the effectiveness of the stipulation to which all parties recently agreed and upon which this court has placed its imprimatur. Defendants' unreasonable refusal to agree upon a statistical formulation of 'statistical variance' cannot be permitted to postpone any longer the relief to which the plaintiffs are entitled under the stipulation and order of June 18, 1973. Therefore, an order will be entered requiring defendants to proceed with the measures outlined in the stipulation."

The order Judge Peckham entered gave the state 20 days to mail out the required letters using the one standard deviation formula and to comply with all the details in the June 1973 order. The judge also ordered the defendants to appear in his courtroom on Monday, July 15, 1973, "to purge themselves of contempt by providing to the court proof of their compliance with the provisions of this order."

The judge made appropriate modifications to the order as well. Recognizing that almost a year had passed, he reduced the three years in the required plans to two years. The most recent numbers provided by the state just days before the contempt hearing indicated that the number 238 districts had been reduced by almost half to 122 districts, due to actions taken by the districts in the preceding 11 months; therefore, the order called for the most recent statistics to be used.

Finally, Judge Peckham refused to dismiss or add districts as parties, finding that the state had the authority to take the actions it had agreed to take and that he had ordered them to take, and that adding any district would not be necessary unless the judge was later asked to cut off funds to a particular district. He also rejected the motion to consolidate: "In view of the fact that full enforcement of the consent decree in this action is now being ordered, while no such decree has been entered in *Larry P. v. Riles*, it is evident that consolidation of the suits would merely generate confusion and delay."

The decision and order by Judge Peckham completely vindicated the positions asserted by Marty, Mo and the CRLA team, and they were elated when the no-nonsense decision came down.

The state, knowing they had no option but to face severe sanctions, promptly complied with the order of the court. It was not powerless to do so after all.

# Chapter 47
## THE REMEDY CAUSED REAL CHANGE

In the following two years, the number of districts with a significant variation continued to dwindle so much that by 1977, the number of districts with significant variance had dropped to 17 according to an affidavit filed by the state. The state also provided copies of various letters sent to the less successful districts and their responses. One response was sent directly to Judge Peckham. It came on the letterhead of an attorney whose office represented the West Covina Valley Unified School District but was signed by the president of the district board. West Covina is a medium-sized district some 20 miles east of downtown Los Angeles. That district advised the judge that the percent of Spanish-surnamed pupils in their classes for the mentally retarded was higher than the percent of Spanish-surnamed pupils in the school population and they were consequently not putting any new Mexican-American children in EMR classes. They asked the judge to change his order to allow them to do so. The district reported that it had created a "waiting list" of Mexican-American students who they had determined to be Educable Mentally Retarded. Rather than violate the court mandate (as they apparently and erroneously believed they otherwise would), they kept students on that list in regular classes instead of placing them "in a program designed to really meet their educational needs." The board president asked the judge how to explain to the parents of Mexican-American children it identified as retarded why their children could not be placed in the EMR classes, given that the district policy was to provide "an educational program which will maximize the intellectual development of each and every student." He concluded by saying, "I believe I understand the motivation behind your ruling, but like many well-intentioned decisions, the remedy appears to be worse than the problem."

Judge Peckham referred the letter to the state with a copy to Al Meyerhoff, one of CRLA's attorneys then responsible for *Diana*. Assistant Attorney General Asher Rubin responded for the state defendants, indicating that the state had been contemplating seeking modification of the order but felt that immediate action to do so was premature and he would so advise the West Covina District.

Meyerhoff, for the plaintiffs, noted that West Covina was the only district to separately write to the court regarding the order, which " . . . is working remarkably well and has substantially corrected the problem of disproportionate placement of Chicano children in EMR classes." He noted 9,000 Mexican-American children had been transitioned out of EMR classes since the 1973 order. Of course, no quota or waiting list had ever been part of the order; thus Meyerhoff suggested the school district take a hard look at the cause of the overrepresentation of Spanish-surnamed students in their EMR classes and evaluate their "present methods of screening and referral used to determine which children of all races are referred for evaluation as to possible evidence of mental retardation." He noted that a San Francisco school official had reported that 90 percent of the referrals in San Francisco had been of children who were racial minorities. His suggestion was that taking these steps would help erase any perceived need for waiting lists.

Progress in West Covina and the other remaining 16 out-of-compliance districts was slow and stubborn. In their mandated explanations for disparity of one standard deviation or more, they advanced several arguments. They argued that the parents of the children assigned to EMR had all consented, so that made it all right. They argued that they no longer had any funds to transition students and that the students would be better off staying where they were. They pointed out that many of their EMR children were in middle school already or in high school, adding to the difficulty of successfully moving them into regular classes. Some simply railed against the idea of having to pay attention to ethnic imbalance. In all fairness, it was not easy to unwind the negative effects of the initial wrongful placements, and so it was not surprising that some problems would persist.

In 1976, again in 1978 and finally in 1981, CRLA lawyers had to prod the state to obtain the required annual statistics, filing further contempt documents and discovery requests. But by 1982, the actions taken by districts over the years had virtually eliminated any statistically significant imbalance in every California school district that had an EMR program.

Because María's mom and Ramón's dad had come forward, critical change had taken place for more than a hundred thousand other children as well as their own.

# Chapter 48
## GROUP IQ TESTS BANNED

Until 1973, it was still the case that public schools were administering so-called group IQ tests to all California school students in the third grade, having apparently learned nothing from the state-acknowledged deficiencies in individual IQ testing. Not surprisingly, the results from the two third-grade standard test batteries—one denominated "IQ" and the other "Achievement"—correlated very highly with each other. Of course, they did: they were really the same animal in a slightly different skin.

The deficiencies and biases that made individual IQ testing and related evaluations unreliable were exacerbated when the test was given simultaneously to a large group of children. The results of these so-called group "IQ tests" were frequently included in student records, creating a stigma that perpetuated teachers' and counselors' beliefs about the students' inability to learn. Both Mexican-American and African American students had disproportionately low scores on these tests. Marty approached the leadership of the California Association of School Psychologists (CASP) to solicit their support for abolition of all test instruments labeled group IQ tests. He gently conveyed that CRLA and other attorneys were prepared to bring suit directly against the association, along with the state if necessary, but that he felt sure that would not be required.

The association leaders and Marty had an extended meeting in Sacramento. No representative of CASP argued that the group tests measured intelligence; indeed, they admitted that they could not do so. The leadership of CASP agreed that the IQ label for a group test was inaccurate and misleading and that they would, internally and externally, support abolition of all group tests denominated "IQ." In 1975, the California legislature removed the authorization for such tests.

# Chapter 49
# NATURE V. NURTURE; THE ROLE OF TESTING

Most everyone agrees that achievement tests are useful and necessary. These tests can and should measure what students have or have not learned at a given point in time. For the following questions: What are the days of the week? What is the square of the number 4? Who was the first president of the United States? The responses should indicate whether the student has learned the answers yet. Designing an educational program to help the student improve in math, history and general knowledge is a fine idea, and the development of tests to assess what students have learned as an aid to that design (and to see how their school is doing generally) makes sense.

A question that should arise if the child does not answer correctly is, Why has the child not achieved the expected level of competence? That a child has been taught in a language he or she does not understand well can provide an answer, or at least a partial answer, to that question. Never having taken a class on American history or having lived their life in a farm labor camp may be another answer to the question. Another answer might be the existence of a learning disability or a behavioral issue caused by stress at home or inadequate instruction, and so on.

IQ tests have been used in the USA and abroad to define minority and immigrant groups as inferior. The belief that certain races had an innate mental inferiority had not disappeared by the early 1970s. In 1969, Arthur Jenson at the University of California suggested in an article that the Head Start Program was probably a waste because his research had found that conceptual ability is inherited, i.e., some portion of one's intelligence is in one's genes and is immutable. He also concluded that African Americans, based on test results that he credited, were genetically of significantly lower intelligence as a group than whites. He based his conclusions on the fact that blacks consistently score about one standard deviation lower than the norm on IQ tests.

Meanwhile at Stanford, William Shockley, a Noble Prize-winner in physics, wrote in 1969 that his research showed that intelligence is entirely hereditary, and blacks are genetically inferior in their capacity to learn. Furthermore, he wrote that those who scored under 100 on IQ tests should be voluntarily sterilized. With this conclusion eugenics was reborn. Shockley based his opinion on the famed English psychologist Cyril Bert and his twin studies. Bert purported to study twins separated at birth and raised in very different environments. He argued in his publications that the intelligence levels of these twins were essentially the same, notwithstanding environmental differences, and that this proved intelligence had to be hereditary. Shockley, Jenson and others took data out of context from so-called "adoption studies." These adoption studies compared the intelligence of adopted children with their parents. The two new eugenicists claimed that the adoption studies showed a low correlation in children with a common environment; this purportedly provided more proof that heredity was the dominant factor in intelligence.

Then in 1974, Princeton psychologist Leon Kamin published *The Science and Politics of IQ*, in which he argued that, "A critical review of the literature produces no evidence which would convince a reasonably prudent man to reject the hypothesis that intelligence test scores have zero heritability." Also in 1974, Kamin presented a paper on his research entitled "Heredity, Intelligence, Politics, and Psychology" and he sent it to Marty along with an expression of his great interest in the *Diana* and *Larry P.* cases. In conversations that ensued between them, Kamin explained his research and indicated his willingness to help as an expert, if needed.

Professor Kamin had spent years delving into the twin studies and particularly the work of Cyril Bert and the generally expressed view among many psychologists that intelligence was 80% the product of genes and 20% environment. Kamin had carefully reviewed the underlying data on which Bert had relied in his separated-at-birth twin studies and demonstrated that Bert had deliberately manipulated his data so it would reflect his desired hypothesis, thereby rendering his entire study scientifically useless. Kamin also demonstrated similar and deep flaws in other studies conducted on twins.

Kamin published a painstaking review of the adopted children studies. After proving critical shortcomings in the methodology and data in those studies, he noted that, if anything, they proved the opposite. The data actually demonstrated there was a close correlation in the test results achieved by natural children and adopted children sharing the same parents, evidence that suggested the stronger role played by environment. Professor Kamin was ultimately one of the twenty-six expert witnesses who testified in the *Larry P.* case trial.

In his prolific work over the years since his initial publications, Dr. Kamin continued to argue there is no scientific support for the notion that intelligence is inherited at all. In both the *Larry P.* and *Diana* cases, Dr. Kamin's research and testimony was used to seriously question the entire premise on which IQ is based, i.e. that it is fixed and therefore can be accurately measured with a one-time standardized test.

# Chapter 50
## THE *LARRY P.* TRIAL

In 1972, after the issuance of the preliminary injunction had been appealed, Armando Menocal assumed the leadership of the *Larry P.* case, including the appeal and later the trial. He was the former head of the Mission office of SFNLAF. Armando joined CRLA as a litigation director in 1972 and remained there until mid-1974. He then joined the highly regarded San Francisco public interest law firm Public Advocates (founded by Bob Gnaizda and three lawyers from other Bay Area legal services), and continued to pilot *Larry P.* from Public Advocates through its trial in 1977.

On December 13, 1974, the *Larry P.* class was modified and expanded to include African American children "who may in the future be classified as mentally retarded on the basis of IQ tests," and the preliminary injunction was expanded to preclude use of tests "which do not properly account for the cultural background or experiences of these children."

In January 1975, the state placed a voluntary moratorium on the IQ testing of children for EMR placement in light of the passage of an experimental Master Plan for special education. That did not forestall the litigation, and intensive discovery commenced in *Larry P.* with depositions taken of the officials in the Department of Education responsible for special education as well as depositions of the class members and their parents.

The California Department of Education's change in attitude from proactive cooperation in 1970 to complete resistance by mid-1973 in *Diana* had become unrelenting by the time *Larry P.*

was active. The case turned into a fully contested battle. Also in 1973, the California Association of Black Psychologists (CABP) reaffirmed its view that no remedy of anything less than complete abolition of the biased IQ tests would be acceptable; compromise was not even on the table.

At trial, the state offered experts who supported the notion that the tests and their results were proper, that the children with low IQ test scores were better off in separate classes, and that significantly more African American school children than Anglos, in fact, belonged in the Educable Mentally Retarded class. They cited decades of the IQ test results that showed that African Americans scored a standard deviation below whites on all parts of the tests. The defendants took the position that use of the Stanford-Binet and WISC IQ tests should resume unabated.

Armando Menocal, Erica Grubb and William Harris were the Public Advocates trial team, putting on the evidence from the children and their parents. Armando cross-examined all of the non-expert witnesses that the Department of Education called to the stand. Joining the Public Advocates team, on a pro bono basis, were Sam Miller of Morrison & Foerster and Steve Dunham of Palmer Madden. Miller and Dunham and their teams handled the task of dealing with the experts for both sides, which was a significant undertaking. Lowell Johnston of the NAACP Legal Defense & Education Fund also provided valuable help. On August 8, 1977, the United States moved to participate as *amicus curiae* in support of the plaintiffs' children, and that request was granted on August 19, 1977.

The non-jury trial began on October 11, 1977, with Judge Peckham presiding. The case was in trial on and off for seven months. Testimony about IQ tests alone consumed some 10,000 pages of transcript. Renowned African American psychologist Asa Hilliard provided testimony on both the history and the fallacies of IQ testing. As noted, Professor Leon Kamin provided background and criticism, attacking the notion that intelligence is fixed. Experts for the plaintiffs pointed out that in classes for the "severely retarded" there was no disparity by race and that black children raised in the homes of white families scored the same as their Anglo counterparts in those homes.

Menocal felt strongly that, in order to win, it would not be enough to show the disparity statistics, overwhelming as they were. His mission was to prove that there had been intentional discrimination by the top California education officials. At a pivotal moment in the long trial, he was cross-examining Superintendent Riles. Methodically, over some two hours, he hammered away, attempting to elicit from the superintendent concrete responses. He then ended with the bare question, "Do you, Mr. Riles, conclude that significantly more black children are mentally retarded than white children, yes or no?" After Riles tried to dodge the question, Judge Peckham directed the superintendent to answer it. After a long pause, Riles answered with reluctance, "Yes, I do." Armando later remembered, "I looked up and saw an expression of disbelief on Judge Peckham's face and knew we had crossed an important threshold."

Although the trial was completed in mid-May 1978, the decision of the court, reported at 495 F. Supp. 926 (N.D. Cal. 1979), did not issue until October 1979. The judge had had a mass of materials to pour over in considering and then in formulating his decision. Indeed, a 150-page addendum, "Findings of Fact", accompanied the formal opinion in the case.

Judge Peckham's opinion was a *tour de force,* and a full report of it is beyond the scope of this story. But some of the evidence and testimony, and certainly the result, stemmed directly from and related directly to *Diana.* In his written opinion, Judge Peckham explicitly found deliberate segregation and discrimination in violation of a host of rights, including the right to equal protection under the laws. In noting that the defendants had been unable to come up with any reason, let alone a compelling reason, for keeping such a disproportionate number of black students in EMR classes, he specifically referenced the fact that these same defendants had twice in *Diana* agreed to eliminate such disparities for Hispanic students. So why should it be different for black students?

With clear displeasure, the judge recited that the defendants had insisted on putting the plaintiff children on the witness stand.

They had attempted in cross-examination to prove that all of these children were deficient mentally after all, and thus no wrong had been done. The state had furthermore argued that these children, given their lack of mental capacity, could not be adequate representatives of the class of black students wrongfully placed in EMR classes. The judge explicitly rejected and criticized those arguments, finding that none of the plaintiff children were, in fact, "mentally retarded."

Judge Peckham found in favor of the plaintiff children and their parents and the class they represented, and he enjoined the defendants from "utilizing, permitting the use of or approving the use of any standardized intelligence tests, including those now approved . . . for the identification of black EMR children or their placement into EMR classes, without securing prior approval of this court."

Back in 1973, Assistant Attorney General Asher Rubin had objected that, if the state made good on promises to require plans, goals and timetables from individual districts for elimination of significant variances for Mexican-American children, those districts might next be required to do the same for African American students. Some six years later, that was exactly what happened. Judge Peckham noted in setting forth the remedy, "Defendants have shown a lack of a compelling interest [in non-action] by agreeing to eliminate such disparities for Hispanic children [in *Diana*]."

Using the *Diana* stipulation and order as a model, Peckham ordered identical procedures in *Larry P.* He imposed the measure of significant variance of one standard deviation, as in *Diana*, and he ordered the re-evaluation of every African American child in an EMR class; he ordered that the same letters be sent to those districts with a significant variance, as had been sent in *Diana*, and the adoption of a three-year plan to eliminate the disparities, as well as to secure explanations from districts who failed. Once again, he ordered supplementary assistance for students transitioning from EMR to regular classes, just as he had ordered for the Mexican-American children some six years earlier.

The results after the entry of Judge Peckham's order, however, were mixed. With monitoring by Public Advocates attorneys, the disparity did drop by about half, but further progress remained stubborn. Recall that for Mexican-American students, they had scored considerably higher on the non-verbal or performance section of the IQ tests than on the verbal parts and, taking advantage of that fact, the CRLA attorneys were able to obtain both a court order and new legislation that completely banned all new placement of second language students who scored above 70 on the non-verbal section of the IQ test into EMR classes. Thus, with the *Diana* case remedy, use of that part of IQ tests continued, stemming the flow of Mexican-American children into the EMR classes while the misplaced were being systematically removed and progress was achieved. But the final order in *Larry P.* was abolition of IQ tests for any purpose, including blocking admission to EMR for a student who would have scored over the cut-off. While this was an important victory, a by-product was that districts could assign new African American students to EMR classes even while they were removing the previous ones improperly placed there, and it was very difficult to monitor this practice. (It is important to note that the IQ test data for African American children at the time showed little difference in their scores between the verbal and non-verbal sections of the culturally biased IQ tests. Therefore, the remedy in *Diana* of only using the non-verbal parts of the IQ test would not work as a solution in *Larry P.*; the entire test would have to have been used for that purpose.)

# PART SIX

# 2018 AND BEYOND
# TODAY AND TOMORROW

# Chapter 51
## REVISITING THE SOLEDAD CHILDREN YEARS LATER

In 2005 and again in 2017, Hector, still seeing clients regularly for CRLA fifty years after he started, made efforts to locate the adults who had been children in the Soledad EMR class. Marty and Mo wanted to learn as much as possible about what had happened to the Soledad Children in the decades since they had been returned to regular classes in the Soledad schools.

Marty, Mo and Hector met with Manual Reyes in 2005. Manuel proudly told them in their first meeting that, after years of trying, he had just passed the examination to become a member of the police force in Soledad. He reported that he did not remember getting much extra help from the Soledad school after he had been taken out of the EMR classroom.

Lucky for me, I was a star baseball player and that gave me some recognition and friends. It helped me to understand that I had never really been retarded. I never did all that well in junior high school, except in math and reading 'cause I liked and understood math and I liked to read, even in English. I dropped out when a teacher told me I would never graduate.

I got a job working in the grape vineyards around Soledad and over twenty years I worked my way up to being a supervisor. It had always been my ambition to become a police officer. I married Angelica, and she was the angel I needed to finish turning my life around. She encouraged me to return to school and work hard to pursue my dream. I got my high school diploma and then went to the Soledad Police Academy. The teachers there also encouraged me, and I completed the classes, got my certificate and applied to join the Soledad Police Department. I had to pass written tests the Soledad Police give to qualify. So I studied hard for that test and I did it.

My greatest pride is helping what we call "adverse youths." It is about kids who get in trouble with the police in the Salinas Valley. They aren't necessarily bad kids, but unless they make a real change in their ways, they will likely end up in prison. I decided to start a program to teach them the grim reality of life in prison, where they are going to end up if they stay on the path they are on. In the program for adverse kids who have gotten in their first round of trouble, we actually take them to prisons. We take the boys to visit the Correctional Facility at Soledad and take the girls to visit the prison for women in Tehachapi. These adverse youths have a chance to get inside the prison and see the individual cells prisoners are kept in. They talk with the inmates who tell them how bad prison is. It makes an unforgettable impression. I think we have helped a lot of kids change their ways. Because someone high up liked what I was doing, they awarded me the California Distinguished Officer Award.

By 2017, Manuel had finished his career as a Soledad policeman and retired from the force, but he still works as a part-time security officer. Manuel ended by saying, "Thank you both so much. If I had been left in that EMR class for the rest of my school years in Soledad, thinking of myself as worthless, I doubt that any of what has happened with my life would have been possible. And you should know there are countless others in California who may not know who you are, but they are thankful that something changed, somehow."

In 2005, Marty, Mo and Hector also met up with Ramón Racio, whose father had been one of the initiators of the *Diana* case. Ramón echoed that it had been difficult for him to catch up in most subjects when he transferred to his new classroom, despite the extra help. He liked math and was good at it, but ultimately dropped out of high school.

Ramón gave a rundown of his career:

I got my regular license to drive cars and it was easy after that to get my commercial driver license because I had already learned what I needed from my dad and my uncles. So, not long after I dropped out of high school, I began my career as a long-haul truck driver, taking loads across the country. I hauled all manner of things: car carriers, refrigerated items, even live animals. After a few years, I was told that there was better pay if I could qualify to carry toxic materials but that it required passing some special extra tests. So I studied and passed easily. And after that, I often transported large trucks with loads of highly hazardous materials that had to be calibrated exactly right by the driver, me, to minimize any possibility of a catastrophic accident. These calculations have to be very precise to avoid risk of explosion or leak or other disaster. And, they are very careful about who they allow to do it. I did it without ever a problem for many years. Not bad, huh, for a retard.

Hector reported that Arturo went to college and might have been a college graduate; he had worked as a high-level supervisor for a major Monterey County company. When approached by Hector in 2005, Arturo had politely but firmly declined to be interviewed and relive his days of segregation.

María was contacted in 2005 by Hector, and when she and her husband met with Marty in his office in San Francisco, it became immediately clear that they were very angry. Apparently, they had been told by some person or persons in Soledad that the other plaintiffs in the *Diana* case had received very large sums of money for damages. They were convinced that everyone else had been paid their share but that the lawyers had kept the amounts due to María. The husband did the talking, getting louder as he went.

"Where is our money?" he asked. "We want it now."

Marty explained that there never had been any damages of any kind and that CRLA in fact had many restrictions against bringing lawsuits for money.

The explanation fell on deaf ears. "You're lying!" María's husband yelled.

"I don't lie," said Marty as he rose, and the two men stared hard at each other, faces less than a foot apart. "There never was any money, and money is not what the case was ever about. Whoever told you that is the liar." Marty continued, "There were more than 13,000 wrongly labeled Educable Mentally Retarded Mexican-American students in classes like the one in Soledad that María was in. . . . And the case was about getting them out and stopping the state from putting other children in those classes who were not developmentally disabled, including María's brothers and sisters. Your wife and her mother are the true heroes for starting this whole case and standing up for María's rights. We only want to recognize her and celebrate what she did."

María looked down as she listened but still did not say anything.

Her husband stood back a bit and said, "She was injured by those people in Soledad. What they did is not right, and she should have been paid for it. She still suffers from what they did and how much she never learned." After several moments of silence, he said, "Whether or not there was money before, unless you pay us now, we have nothing more to say."

They got up and Marty walked them to the elevator, saying that he understood their feelings. He agreed that María had been injured and that Soledad should have paid for it, but repeated that there were no damages nor money to pay.

"I hope you'll reconsider," Marty said.

They did not.

Manuel reported that the twins, Diana and Armando, had not adjusted well, had dropped out early and moved away. No one had information on the lives or whereabouts of Rachel, Ernesto or Margarita after they and their families had left Soledad for good.

At an education conference in 2000, Marty was approached by one of the articulate conference speakers, a Mexican American with a Master's degree. She thanked him effusively, saying she had been in an EMR class in Southern California when she was in second and third grades; getting removed from that class had changed the course of her life.

On another occasion, Mo met an attorney, Alejandro Matuk, born in Monclova in the state of Coahuila, Mexico. Alejandro came to the United States in 1957 and was enrolled initially in a class for the Educable Mentally Retarded in the Orchardale Elementary School in Whittier, California. He did not speak any English at the time but knew that his placement was not right. Fortunately, he was removed after only one year and, once he learned English, he had no further issues. He later graduated from California State at Fullerton and then the University of Michigan Law School. Today this wrongly labeled "mentally retarded" student practices law in San Diego.

An equally talented and bright Mexican American, Carlos Bowker, was not so fortunate when he relied on the El Centro school system for an education. Carlos told Mo: "I spent my first eleven years of life in Jalisco, Mexico, and joined my mother and stepfather in El Centro on Brighton Avenue in the poor part of town. We all spoke only Spanish. In the fall, I went to Wilson Junior High School. My teacher did not speak Spanish and seemed to have no idea what to do with me, so she just gave me a stack of "5 x 7" cards with pictures on them and an English name under them, like 'ball' and 'dog.' It was easy enough to learn those but with no other real instruction, I pretty much skipped school when I could. When I got to high school, I was taken into a test room, where a man who spoke no Spanish gave me some kind of test. I could not really even understand the questions he was asking, and a few days later, they put me in an EMR classroom with about 25 other students—white, Latino and black.

"I was on the road to nowhere. I worked for a car dealer washing cars and then as a migrant farmworker all over California. My lucky break came when I heard about the Neighborhood Youth Corp, a part of the War on Poverty. I went there and the group leader, Porsha Thompson, encouraged me to go to real school. I graduated from Imperial Valley College and then attended San Jose State. CRLA hired me as a community worker. Later, I worked in Sacramento for the Border Development Corporation, the California Labor Relations Board and the Department of Fair Employment and Housing. Then Attorney General, now Governor Brown, hired me as lead investigator for his Underground Economy Unit, and I have been working on wage claims and citizenship representations ever since. I got hundreds, if not thousands, of workers their proper pay and have helped thousands of immigrants qualify to become citizens. I was extremely lucky to escape the fate that improper placement in an Educable Mentally Retarded class had me destined for. I know others left in there were not so fortunate, and I can't thank CRLA enough for attacking this terrible practice."

# Chapter 52
# *DIANA* AND *LARRY P.* DECADES LATER

Both the *Diana* and *Larry P.* cases were written about and commented upon extensively; they came to be described as landmark cases. *The Handbook of Multicultural School Psychology: An Interdisciplinary Perspective* cites *Diana* as "perhaps the most influential court case concerning assessment practices for [the] bilingual population of children." Both cases have been important precedents for the evaluation of testing and test instruments, as well as cases brought on behalf of the handicapped.

As time has passed, the literature reflects important debates among psychologists and academics as to the best practices going forward for the assessment and the education of low-performing students. In that context, there are some who have criticized the remedies in the court orders issued in *Diana* and *Larry P.*, and a few indeed purport to offer empirical data to demonstrate that the cases were either incorrectly decided or went too far. Those critics presuppose, however, that there was an alternative for the Mexican-American and African American students at that time, an appropriate place for them to be. In fact, there were no quality alternative programs for those children to help them catch up to their cohort, no classes that would have been better than their regular classes. Indeed, taking part in regular classes was important for their socialization; they would make friends and wouldn't endure the schoolyard taunts. The critics also seem to assume the absence of racial and cultural bias in those responsible for determining the academic fate of the children.

At least at the time of both *Diana* and *Larry P.* the evidence was overwhelming that the "special" classes to which more than 20,000 students were assigned without cause were dead-end warehouses for them. They provided very little learning to these students and to the hundreds of thousands of students who would have faced a similar fate. The evidence is unshakable. Too many state and local officials believed that high numbers of black and Mexican-American children were genetically inferior or, in any event, needed to be segregated out of the general student population. School psychologists, who should have and did know better, enabled the shuffling off of generations of minority children into the poverty and illiteracy that came with their lack of any meaningful education. Drastic remedies were essential to halt what was going on; anything less would have been far too little. For the most part these legal remedies worked.

Judge Peckham, after a decade of monitoring the *Diana* case and finding the State of California in contempt of court, and then sitting through months of trial in the *Larry P.* case, wrote as follows:

> The history of this litigation has demonstrated the failure of legislators and administrative agencies to confront problems that clearly had to be faced, and it has revealed an all-too-typical willingness either to do nothing or to pass on issues to the courts. . . . Educators have too often been able to rationalize inaction by blaming educational failure on an assumed intellectual infirmity of disproportionate numbers of children. That assumption, without validation, is unacceptable, and it is made all the more invidious when 'legitimated' by ostensibly neutral, scientific IQ scores.

His orders in both cases abruptly changed the lives of hundreds of thousands of young children.

The rights of English as a second-language and children of color in school systems, public and private, remain far from guaranteed. The ability of these children and others who lack resources to hire effective counsel to, in Judge Peckham's words, "pass on" issues to the courts when necessary remains critical. Attacks by powerful vested interests on CRLA and other legal services programs, which attempt to quash or unduly restrict their work has never ceased and never will, so long as they are challenging inequity, whether in the school system, on the worksite, in the polling place, in the provision of public services or in housing and transportation equity. The next generation of Dianas and Larry P.s, and the estimated fourteen million Americans living now below the poverty line, depend on free and effective representation that will fight to preserve their ability to achieve and prosper. They deserve no less.